# In the Land of Ur

*Also by Hans Baumann*

    The Caves of the Great Hunters
    The World of the Pharaohs
    Gold and Gods of Peru
    Lion Gate and Labyrinth

# In the Land of Ur

*The Discovery of Ancient Mesopotamia*

*by* HANS BAUMANN
*Translated by Stella Humphries*

PANTHEON BOOKS

*English translation* © *Copyright 1969 by Random House, Inc.*
*and Oxford University Press.*
*All rights reserved under International*
*and Pan-American Copyright Conventions.*
*Published in the United States by Pantheon Books,*
*a division of Random House, Inc., New York.*
*and in London, England by Oxford University Press.*
*Library of Congress Catalog Card Number: 77-77434*
*Manufactured in the United States of America*
*by The Book Press, Brattleboro, Vt.*
*Color inserts printed by Rae Publishing Co., Inc., Cedar Grove, N.J.*
*Originally published in German as Im Lande Ur*
© *1968, by Sigbert Mohn Verlag*

**Baumann, Hans,** 1914–
    In the Land of Ur; the discovery of ancient Mesopotamia.
Translated by Stella Humphries. [New York] Pantheon
Books [1969]
    166 p. illus. (part col.), map. 22 cm. 4.95

    Describes archaeological finds in Mesopotamia and what they have revealed of the ancient civilizations of that area.
Translation of Im Lande Ur.

    1. Mesopotamia—Antiquities. 2. Civilization, Assyro-Babylonian.
[1. Mesopotamia—Antiquities. 2. Civilization, Assyro-Babylonian. 3. Archaeology] I. Title.

DS69.5.B3513    1969b        913.3′5′03        77–77434
                                                                     MARC
Trade Ed.: ISBN: 0-394-80807-X    Lib. Ed.: ISBN: 0-394-90807-4

# Contents

| | |
|---|---|
| A Discovery in Uruk | 1 |
| Adventures and Good Luck | 6 |
| The Men Who Deciphered Cuneiform | 22 |
| Gods in the Land of Ur | 34 |
| The Creation of Paradise | 47 |
| Gilgamesh Protests | 57 |
| The Secret of Ur | 70 |
| Temple Towers | 80 |
| Of Farmers, Builders, and Others | 88 |
| Of Schools and Scribes | 95 |
| Tricks, Forgeries, and Practical Jokes | 103 |
| Uruk and Aratta | 112 |
| The Quarrel over the Garden of Eden | 118 |
| A King of the Oppressed | 125 |
| Akkad, the New City | 131 |
| Gudea, Builder of Temples | 140 |
| The Winged Horse | 148 |

*Appendices:*

WORDS, PLACES, AND PEOPLE  *153*
FAMOUS MESOPOTAMIAN EXPLORERS  *161*
MAJOR EXCAVATIONS IN CHRONOLOGICAL ORDER  *163*
CHRONOLOGICAL TABLE WITH NAMES OF KINGS  *165*

In the Land of Ur

# A Discovery in Uruk

Mesopotamia, the land between two rivers, is mostly desert today. Hardly anything grows in the yellow earth deposited by the Euphrates and the Tigris since time immemorial, and the miserable vegetation that sprouts after the rains have fallen is burned to a cinder by the sun during the summer months. Clouds of sand drift lazily across the plains and, much more rarely, a camel caravan painfully makes its way. When the sun sinks below the horizon and the afterglow has faded, the jackals start to howl.

In this wilderness the only landmarks are huge, shapeless mounds, looming eerily into the night, or standing desolate and abandoned by day. Over them reigns Death.

It was not always so. Once there were thriving communities in the Land of the Two Rivers. For thousands of years, men built fine cities, splendid with temples and palaces. Now they have become mounds of rubble that the Bedouin call *tells.* Mighty edifices have vanished within such *tells,* taking with them their carvings and statues, precious vessels and jewelry and royal thrones. The wind and the rain have gnawed away at stout walls and columns made of mud brick. When the days of the kings were over, gardens of paradise reverted to desert, and fabulous cities crumbled into heaps of debris almost overnight.

For more than one hundred years, archaeologists from all over the world have been coming to this region to explore these mounds, and their amazing discoveries have roused ever-increas-

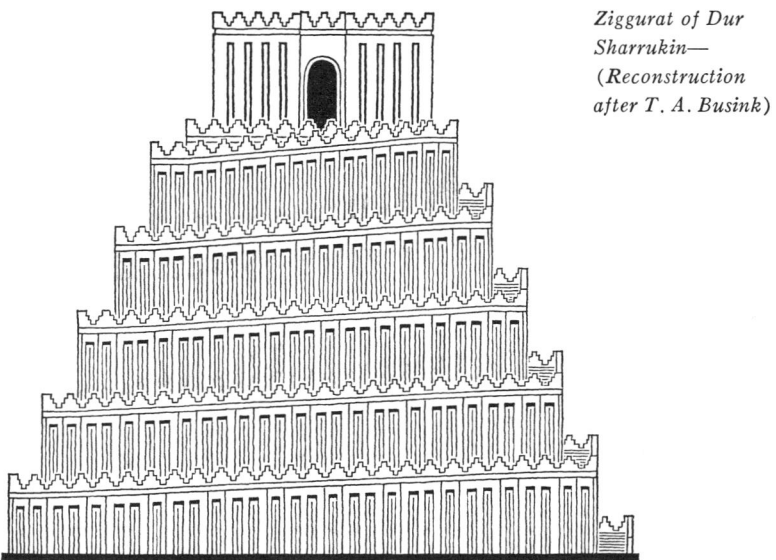

*Ziggurat of Dur Sharrukin—
(Reconstruction after T. A. Busink)*

ing admiration. Today, thanks to them, we know who built these antique cities and what their names were.

One of the most ancient royal capitals was known as Uruk. It lay hidden for thousands of years in a hill that the Arabs call Warka. In the winter of 1958–59, a team of German archaeologists discovered the remains of a wall that had been built not long after the death of Alexander the Great. Beneath this wall there was found a jug dating from the same era. Its neck was missing but the hole at the top had been carefully closed with a lid, and this lid was some twenty-five hundred years older than the jug itself. When the lid was lifted, there was an alabaster figurine inside, with eyeballs of white pearl inset with pupils of lapis lazuli.

Both the statuette and the lid belonged to the same period, that is, they were not far short of five thousand years old. The little figure is that of a bearded man wearing a round, close-fitting cap. His hands are clasped to his breast in prayer, a worshiper who stands before his god in fear and trembling.

The team conducting the excavation had seen figures like this before, although admittedly none had been known hitherto from such an early period. In ancient Mesopotamia, men and women often had small images of this type made in their own likeness, to be placed inside their temples. It was a common practice, especially for kings, who combined the roles of prince and priest. For the men who discovered it, this statuette had a tale to tell. From old inscriptions that had already been deciphered, they knew the kind of prayer that such a king might utter. When a certain priest-prince of Lagash was about to build a new temple, this was how he addressed his god:

Look upon me and my life will be lengthened. I hear what you say to me. On the day I start to build a new temple, a wind shall arise, heralding the rain, announcing that water will fall from heaven in great abundance. The fields will bring forth a rich harvest, the waters will rise in ditches and canals. In the Land

*Old Sumerian statuette of an ensi, in a jug (after Lenzen)*

of Sumer, oil will be poured out abundantly, wool will be weighed in abundance. On the day when I begin the restoration of your temple, you will set your foot upon the mountains from which the storm comes. And you will send a wind that will breathe the breath of life into the land.

Long life for the Land of Sumer and for himself—these were the gifts the worshiper asked his god to grant. As he calls upon him, the glory of the Eternal is reflected so strongly on his face that the onlooker too is moved by its power.

This statuette comes from one of the earliest periods in the history of the Land of Sumer, or the Land of Ur as it is often called. This is the "country of origin" of so many things that we take for granted as indispensable features of civilization. In those earliest times, "the gods bequeathed the earth to mankind," as Dr. Walter Andrae, who was responsible for excavating Ashur, once put it.

But how did the little "worshiper" come to be placed in a jug that was manufactured twenty-five hundred years later? There is an explanation for this, too.

When Alexander died, one of his successors decided to build a new temple on the foundations of an old one, and the workmen came upon the statuette among the debris. And they too, the "first finders," were so struck by the aura of holiness on the man's face that they could not bring themselves to throw it away, beyond the sacred precincts. So they hid it safely inside the jar and reburied it inside the temple confines. Thus it survived for thousands of years to come, with the new walls above it. When it was dug out of the ruins of these later walls for the second time, the figure had lost nothing of its impact. The suppliant was as "alive as on the first day."

The experts in Uruk were able to reconstruct the original history of the small figure they had disinterred so carefully because they were prepared for discoveries like this, and they were in a position to compare one find with another. The first explorers, however, the men who went to dig in the Land of Ur in the middle of the last century, knew nothing at all about the people who had built the oldest cities. They did not even know the name, Sumer. They set out to bring back for their various museums as many valuable specimens as they could find. Their prime aim was to rediscover the lost cities of Babylon and Nineveh, and this they did. They certainly found what they were looking for—indeed they found much more.

# Adventures and Good Luck

In 1808, a young man named Claudius James Rich was appointed British Resident in Baghdad. No one there thought of him as a foreigner, for both in speech and behavior he could pass as a native. He had begun to learn Arabic when he was only nine years old, and later he had acquired several other oriental languages.

Rich paid a short visit to Babylon in the year 1811, and when he left the ancient Land of Babel, he was able to send to London a number of stone carvings and tablets inscribed in cuneiform, the script of the Babylonians. He also included a sketch map covering a large area of the ruins and remains that he had surveyed personally. He presented all his material to the British Museum, where it was exhibited and provoked a good deal of interest. Rich died young, but the book he had written about his journey was given wide recognition after his death, most notably in France.

Some time later, a vacancy arose at the French Consulate in Mosul, the city on the Tigris River, and a famous orientalist, Julius Mohl, suggested to the then French Minister for Foreign Affairs that it should be filled by someone who was interested in archaeology. A certain Paul Émile Botta was the man he had in mind, for Botta was already well acquainted with the Middle East, and he seemed eminently qualified to explore the Mesopotamian ruins. Botta was the son of an Italian historian, he spoke Arabic, and he knew how to deal with the native population. He had great stamina, an adventurous disposition, and his ambition in life was to discover the lost city of Nineveh.

As soon as Botta was appointed he lost no time. He had hardly settled in at Mosul before he began excavating the hill of Kuyunjik, which lies across from Mosul on the opposite bank of the Tigris. This enormous rubbish mound did indeed contain the ruins of Nineveh, but Botta dug there in vain for a whole winter, finding only unimportant remains.

On March 20, 1843, among the Arabs who watched the team at work, there was a dyer from Khorsabad, a village that lay ten miles to the north of Kuyunjik. Observing how Botta examined each fragment of alabaster and brick with minute attention, the Arab told him that "stuff like that" was to be found at every step and turn on the hill of Khorsabad, and there were remnants of large stone statues as well.

At first Botta refused to believe him. He had been misled by natives only too often in the past. But next day, he sent some of his assistants to Khorsabad and very soon a messenger returned confirming the news that the ground there did indeed contain carvings of kings and warriors, and some impressive images of awe-inspiring beasts. When he heard this, Botta set off at once to see for himself. In Khorsabad, he found that some large reliefs had already been uncovered and he made drawings of them. Then he arranged for new trenches to be dug along the inner side of massive walls.

All the men working on the hill of Kuyunjik were now transferred to Khorsabad, and in a matter of days they had brought to light such astonishing remains of palaces that Botta could write to Paris: "I believe I am the first person to have discovered sculptures which can properly be ascribed to the period when Nineveh was in its heyday."

In Paris, and for that matter, throughout the world, people pricked up their ears. Money was sent from France so that Botta could continue his "dig" on a bigger scale, and he got down to work with enthusiasm. For three years he had to contend with difficulties. There were the sheer mass of debris, the lethal climate, the snakes and the vermin, as well as the suspicion of the Arabs; to say nothing of the devious ways of the local pasha, who threatened anyone helping Botta with torture and imprisonment.

A colleague from Paris, the artist Flandin, was sent to join him. Many of the reliefs crumbled to dust as soon as they were exposed to the air, but if they could be copied in time, at least they would be preserved on paper. In this field, Flandin was a supreme master. Fortunately many of the carvings proved to be less fragile because they had not been damaged by fire and so made brittle.

Botta had his spoils loaded onto rafts, but the first consignment foundered to the bottom of the Tigris, a treacherous river known as "the arrow-swift." Most of the other crates were transported by sea, but they had to go the long way round via Bombay. These finds reached France eventually, but when they arrived in Paris, in February 1847, they were in deplorable condition.

*Reliefs from the palace of Sargon II (original drawing by Flandin)*

Nevertheless, the Louvre staged a great exhibition, which included gigantic stone carvings, a black obelisk, reliefs, and clay tablets. They made a deep impression on visitors who came from many lands, and the way for exploring the submerged civilizations of the Land of the Two Rivers had now been opened.

The next important step was taken by an Englishman, Austen Henry Layard, later Sir Henry. He came from an old Huguenot family, and was a man of restless temperament. At the age of twenty-two, with Rich's book on Babylon in his pocket, he set off for the Near East in the company of a friend who wanted to travel to Ceylon overland as far as possible because he was nervous about becoming seasick. Ceylon was also Layard's destination, for an uncle of his had suggested a post for him out there, but the lands of the Near and Middle East exercised such a powerful spell that Layard never reached his goal. He traveled across Asia Minor on horseback, sometimes with others, often alone. He fell gravely ill more than once, was robbed twice, and he was captured in a slave raid by Bedouins. He escaped and turned up at the British Consul's at Damascus, exhausted and half-naked, to seek asylum there.

But Layard did not remain long in Damascus. He was soon off again on horseback, and he paid a visit to Nineveh. He was fascinated by this pitiless country, and the sight of the enormous mounds of rubble beneath which lay buried the cities of Assyria made a deeper impression on him, he said, "than the temples of Baalbek and the theaters of Ionia."

When he stood on the hill of Kuyunjik for the first time in 1840, he made up his mind he would dig there one day. But before that, he traveled farther east still, to see the rock of Behistun where there is a large and ancient inscription in cuneiform carved into the mountainside at a dizzy height.

By the beginning of November he had returned to Mosul, and this time he made a close inspection of two mounds on the opposite bank of the Tigris. One of these hills had a village built on its slopes, and according to the belief of the Arabs, it housed the tomb of Jonah. Jonah was the prophet who had refused to obey God's command to go to Nineveh, and had therefore been swallowed by a great whale and later disgorged. Because of its religious significance to the Arabs, it was clearly taboo for excavation. The other mound, however, was there for anyone who chose to try his luck. Botta had dug there already, but not deeply enough. When Layard approached him, he gladly showed Layard his sketches and plans. The British ambassador in Constantinople was sympathetic too, and he gave Layard sixty pounds from his own pocket. These were literally all the funds Layard had at his disposal to start his first dig. But he did not hesitate. He set out at once, and in his own words, "crossed the mountains of Pontus and the great steppes of Usum Yilak as fast as post-horses could carry me, descended the highlands of the valley of the Tigris, galloped over the vast plains of Assyria, and reached Mosul in twelve days."

All the same, Layard, like Botta, made his first discoveries elsewhere and not in Kuyunjik. Mosul at that time was governed by a pasha known as Keritli Oglu, "the son of the Cretan," although the Arabs were privately convinced that he was the son of Satan. This pasha robbed those whom he should have protected and was notorious for inventing new taxes and new tortures. Once he had his own death announced and then scared the wits out of the population by "coming to life" again. He was thus able to arrest everyone who had rejoiced at the false news and confiscate their property ". . . for spreading rumors endangering the safety of the state." When he sent his minions out to the villages, his instructions to them were simply: "Go, destroy, eat!"

This human monster had one eye and one ear, he was fat and pockmarked and full of guile. So in spite of having a permit from the Turkish government to dig, Layard thought it would not be advisable to begin work in this pasha's territory. Instead he set off one day with three companions for a voyage down the

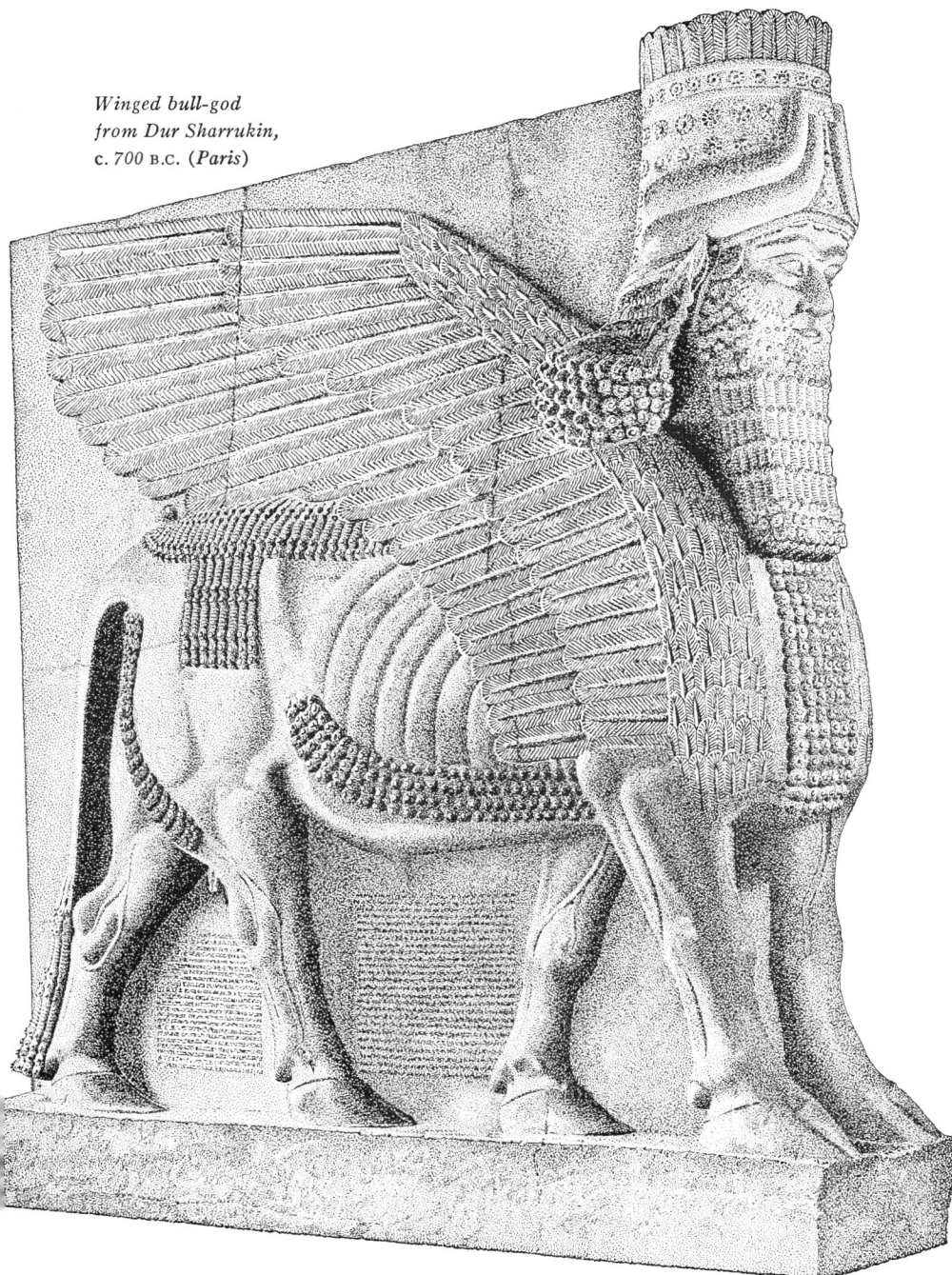

*Winged bull-god from Dur Sharrukin,* c. 700 B.C. (*Paris*)

Tigris. They were all armed with rifles, spears, and other terrifying weapons, ostensibly to hunt wild boar. At sunset, the four men stepped ashore. A village they approached seemed deserted, for the inhabitants had fled from the "one-eyed devil." Only one hovel showed a gleam of firelight, and in it Layard came upon three wizened females, a few naked children, two mangy dogs, and a man named Awad, the sheikh of the Jehesh Bedouin. Awad invited Layard into his hut and when he heard that Layard intended to excavate, he promised to recruit helpers for him. That same night, the sheikh told Layard about King Nimrod, "the mighty hunter," whose marvelous palace, he said, lay buried in the mound of Nimrud close by, as did Nimrod himself.

"It was the same Nimrod whom Abraham fought, and the patriarch destroyed the idols the king worshiped," said Awad. "And God came to Abraham's help and sent a gnat which tormented Nimrod so horribly day and night that the great hunter had a room with glass walls built inside his palace to keep the gnat out. But the insect pierced the glass and slipped into the king's left ear. It housed itself inside the king's brain and there it grew and grew, buzzing so loudly that the royal servants had to beat their master's head with hammers to ease his sufferings. His head turned to stone, and it was only after four hundred years of such torture that the mighty hunter who had incurred the wrath of God was able to die."

This was the tale that Awad told. Next morning he went off and returned presently with six Arabs, all members of his own tribe, who were prepared to assist Layard. On the very first day of the dig, ten alabaster slabs came to light as well as a number of inscriptions, but at every turn they found the remains of walls. Two royal palaces were struck on that first day, and after a few weeks, they discovered also the remains of a brick *ziggurat,* or temple tower constructed in tiers or terraces. The excavators found reliefs of first-class workmanship, depicting soldiers and war chariots, horses and gods, and many prisoners who were being treated with savage cruelty. These carvings described battles and triumphal feasts, they told the story of the Assyrian people who "delighted in war." This was the nation the prophets of Israel had cursed for their barbaric deeds.

Layard recruited more helpers still and hurried on with the excavation. Then soldiers appeared with orders from Keritli Oglu to stop the work at once. According to the pasha, there were True Believers buried in the mound and their rest must not be disturbed. Layard, who had seen no signs of a Moslem cemetery, rode off to Mosul at once. The one-eyed pasha assured him of his friendship, but declared that he could not be responsible if the desecration of Moslem graves provoked the anger of the local Arabs.

On his return to Nimrud, Layard won the confidence of the captain of the troop, who confessed to the Englishman: "We had orders from Keritli Oglu to remove gravestones from Arab cemeteries under cover of night, and to do this, we had to disturb more genuine graves than we could build sham ones in Nimrud. For we had to hurry, and in our haste we lost many of the accursed stones, half-killing ourselves and our horses in the bargain."

Layard now had two reliable allies. He was able to ride to Constantinople in order to ask for permits of greater authority for his excavations and he was successful in obtaining them. Money was sent to him from the British Museum in London, together with instructions "to deliver the greatest possible number of finds in the shortest possible time." The one-eyed pasha was finally scotched. His misgovernment had gone to such lengths that it led to his own undoing and he was deposed.

At the end of October, Layard returned to the hill of Nimrud. A hut of mud bricks and twigs was built for him, but before the roof was complete, a shower of rain fell and the walls were so thoroughly saturated that stray seeds of grass in the mud began to germinate. Throughout the winter, the inner walls of the hut were overgrown with grass. Round about the hill, friendly Arabs pitched their black tents. They watched over Layard and they helped him.

The person who was to become his most important assistant

*Wounded lion, from the palace of King Ashurbanipal, Nineveh (London)*

was a seventeen-year-old Chaldean named Hormuzd Rassam. His reputation spread quickly through the desert. "He sees what lies in the earth," they said of him; and it was a fact that his luck as an excavator was quite fantastic.

On the instructions of the British Museum, Layard was to remove no more than was absolutely essential for lifting out carvings, sculptures, and the like. Then the trenches were to be filled in again, whereby much was totally destroyed. The number of trophies, however, was enormous. There were the keepers of the gates, gigantic stone figures shaped like winged lions and bulls with human heads. There were reliefs with scenes of fighting and hunting, vessels and vases, ivory carvings, bronze implements, weapons, and inscriptions.

One day in November, as Layard was returning to the mound after a visit to the camp of a friendly sheikh named Abd-ur-Rahman, two Arabs came riding toward him at full gallop. From afar off they shouted: "Hasten, O Bey! . . . for they have found Nimrod himself! His stone head is already peering from the ground. We have seen him with our own eyes!"

The mound was swarming with Arabs. As Layard dismounted, Awad stepped out of a newly opened trench and asked for a present, which was the custom when an exceptional find was made. Then the workmen pulled aside a makeshift screen to reveal a colossal alabaster head. The face was perfectly preserved and on the head was a cap with three horns. Sheikh Abd-ur-Rahman had heard the news and he came galloping up with half his tribe. At the sight of the head, he exclaimed: "This is not the work of men's hands, but of the infidel giants—higher than the date trees. This is one of the idols that Noah cursed before the Flood!" And he gazed at the huge stone image in fascinated horror.

Layard, however, had sheep slaughtered and the musicians summoned and a great feast was held, during which Abd-ur-Rahman made a memorable speech: "God is great! God is great! Here are stones that have been buried ever since the time of Holy Noah. . . . Perhaps they were underground before the deluge. I have lived on these lands for years. My father, and the father of my father, pitched their tents here before me; but they never heard of these figures. For twelve hundred years have the True Believers . . . been settled in this country and none of them ever heard of a palace underground. Neither did they who went before them. But lo! here comes a Frank from many days' journey off, and he walks up to the very place. Here, he says, is the palace; there, he says, is the gate; and he shows us what has been all our lives beneath our feet without our having known anything about it. Wonderful! Wonderful! Is it by books, or is it by magic, or by your prophets that you have learnt these things? Speak, O Bey! Tell me the secret of wisdom!"

Another feast was held later to celebrate the removal of two winged figures, a lion and a bull. An enormous wagon built with iron axles was sent out from Mosul. They had to dig trenches a hundred feet long, sixteen feet wide and twenty-two feet deep and use rollers in order to remove these stone colossi from the mound and load them onto the wagon. It needed three hundred men to draw it along, and a huge crowd of people gathered beside it, shivering the air with their shrill cries. They all set off in procession, with Layard and the sheikh riding at their head. The drumming of the drummers and the piping of the pipers were drowned in the hullabaloo, while Abd-ur-Rahman's outriders raced up and down, staging mock battles. The risky business of transportation was undertaken by a bankrupt shipping merchant whom Layard had saved from a debtors' prison. The statues were taken up river by raft and all went well.

Victor Place, the man who succeeded Botta in Khorsabad, was not so lucky. He dug there between 1852 and 1855, and of more than two hundred large crates he entrusted to rafts on the Tigris, only twenty-six arrived safely. On May 23, 1855, he was set upon by hostile Arabs at a point not far from the confluence of the Tigris and the Euphrates and during the encounter most of the rafts with their irreplaceable cargo sank into the muddy waters.

Layard's finds, which reached London safely, persuaded the British Museum to place larger sums of money at his disposal. After excavating no less than seven royal palaces at Nimrud, he began to dig where Botta had failed at his first attempt, that is, in the mound of Kuyunjik. This *tell* is almost thirty-three hundred feet long and nearly two thousand feet wide and it rises about a hundred feet above the level of the plains. It has been calculated that a mound of this size must contain some fifteen million tons of rubble and that it would take one thousand people approximately one hundred and twenty-four years to sift the whole of it. These figures reveal the courage of the first excavators in tackling the job—and their extraordinary luck.

There was bitter rivalry between the British and the French over Kuyunjik, and a great explorer, Major Rawlinson, was sent to Mesopotamia to represent the British interests. He made an agreement with Victor Place whereby the mound was divided in two, with the French excavating the northern part and the English concentrating on the south. In December 1853, Layard's assistant, Rassam, had galleries dug secretly which penetrated the French sector. Inside them Rassam found some magnificent carvings representing the royal lion hunts. Bluntly he claimed possession of this part of the site and he absolutely refused to budge. Thus the finds from the two most beautiful of the Assyrian palaces, those of the kings Sennacherib and Ashurbanipal, landed in London instead of the Louvre. On his second excavation in Kuyunjik, Layard discovered sixty palace chambers, two thousand reliefs, twenty seven portals, and ten winged bulls.

There was no longer any doubt about it, Nineveh had been found. At two places, considerable portions of a royal library came to light, comprising many thousands of cuneiform tablets. True, neither Layard nor Rassam could read these tablets. For them they were just so many more museum curios to be exhibited, collections of tablets that looked as if birds had strutted across the clay when it was wet. They were shoveled into baskets and crates and many of them broke as they were being handled. Nevertheless, these inscriptions had been wrested from their hiding place and were available for deciphering later.

During the years that followed, Rassam showed his incomparable intuition at a number of different sites. In Balawat, he discovered a gateway inlaid with bronze strips on which were embossed pictures of battle scenes, the Bronze Gates of Balawat. Rassam sent a larger number of treasures to London than any other excavator, but he went about his work more like a grave robber than a scientist. When he could not supervise a site personally, he appointed Arab foremen who were almost invariably ignorant tribesmen. He discovered one rich site after another and he handed them over in turn to his assistants with the instructions: "Look, rummage, find!"

But Botta, too, had had no compunction about sawing up figures of winged bulls because they were too heavy for the transport available. Even Layard took little care in handling the most precious objects the mound of Kuyunjik produced, namely the archives, because at first he believed these clay tablets were

*Camp scene from Nineveh, c. 700 B.C. (Berlin)*

pieces of "decorated pottery"!

These early archaeologists lived in worse conditions than the conquerors of Nineveh, according to one of their number. They unearthed more than all those who came after them, stated others. Botta and Layard, Rassam and Place and their immediate successors, were exploring virgin territory. They had to rely on their own resources, for there was no one who could teach them; and they had to face far greater obstacles than later explorers. Rubbish heaps of intimidating dimensions loomed up before them, and there were no signposts to say: "This is where Nineveh stood," or "Babylon was here." Yet nothing could deter these men from getting down to work in the desert and carrying it through to the end. So they were pioneers and blazed a trail, even if their crude methods destroyed a great deal of value. They were born excavators and the Land of the Two Rivers drew them like a magnet, as if they were native sons of the region. They found the lost cities they sought with such assurance that they might have been travelers returning home.

They grasped the essentials, too. Layard writes of the stone guardians of the gates in these terms:

What more sublime images could have been borrowed from nature by men who sought . . . to embody their conception of the wisdom, power, and ubiquity of a Supreme Being? They could find no better type of intellect and knowledge than the head of the man; of strength, than the body of the lion; of ubiquity, than the wings of the bird.

These winged human-headed lions were not idle creations, the offspring of mere fancy; their meaning was written upon them. . . . Through the portals which they guarded, kings, priests, and warriors had borne sacrifices to their altars . . . and furnished its mythology with symbols long recognized by the Assyrian votaries . . .

These earliest excavators inspired others. Many trod in their wake, and their successors learned how to read what was written on the tablets found in the palaces of Nineveh, Khorsabad, and Nimrud.

In the spring of 1953, the British archaeologist Professor M. E. L. Mallowan was digging in Nimrud and he came upon a well which Layard had searched many years before. But Layard had not investigated deeply enough, so it seems. Mallowan cleared the well right down to the bottom, which lay about eighty feet below ground level. And there, buried in the mud, were sixteen ivory tablets and seven of walnut wood. They were writing boards, covered with a wax overlay. Marks at the edges revealed that the tablets had once been held together with hinges to make a kind of folding book. The cover of the book was found too, bearing a title that showed it had been a guide to the meaning of astrological omens. A thorough examination indicated that the hinges, which were probably made of gold, had been wrenched out by force. And subsequently, intensive research threw light on how the book had found its way into the well.

It must have been in the year 703 B.C. It was then that the Assyrian king, Sargon II, who had moved the royal residence from Nineveh to Khorsabad, had met his death in battle. His son and heir, Sennacherib, had quarreled bitterly with his father, and his hatred of his sire was so far-reaching that he had everything destroyed that reminded him of Sargon. He attacked Babylon, to which his father had shown favor, and he re-established Nineveh as his capital. Sargon's citadel in Khorsabad was walled up on Sennacherib's orders and Sargon's palace in Nimrud was handed over to the soldiers to plunder. Thus the "folding book" came into the hands of the armed mob. None of the looters could read, so they pulled out the gold hinges and threw the book into the well. The tablets recovered in 1953 could tell the world about this episode from the last years of the Babylonian-Assyrian empire because the archaeologists who found them were better trained than Botta or Layard. They could read cuneiform, whose traces they discerned on the waxen remains of the folding book. But scholars had found the key to deciphering the ancient languages of Mesopotamia long before the discovery of the "Book in the Well," and their achievements are no less important than those of the earliest explorers.

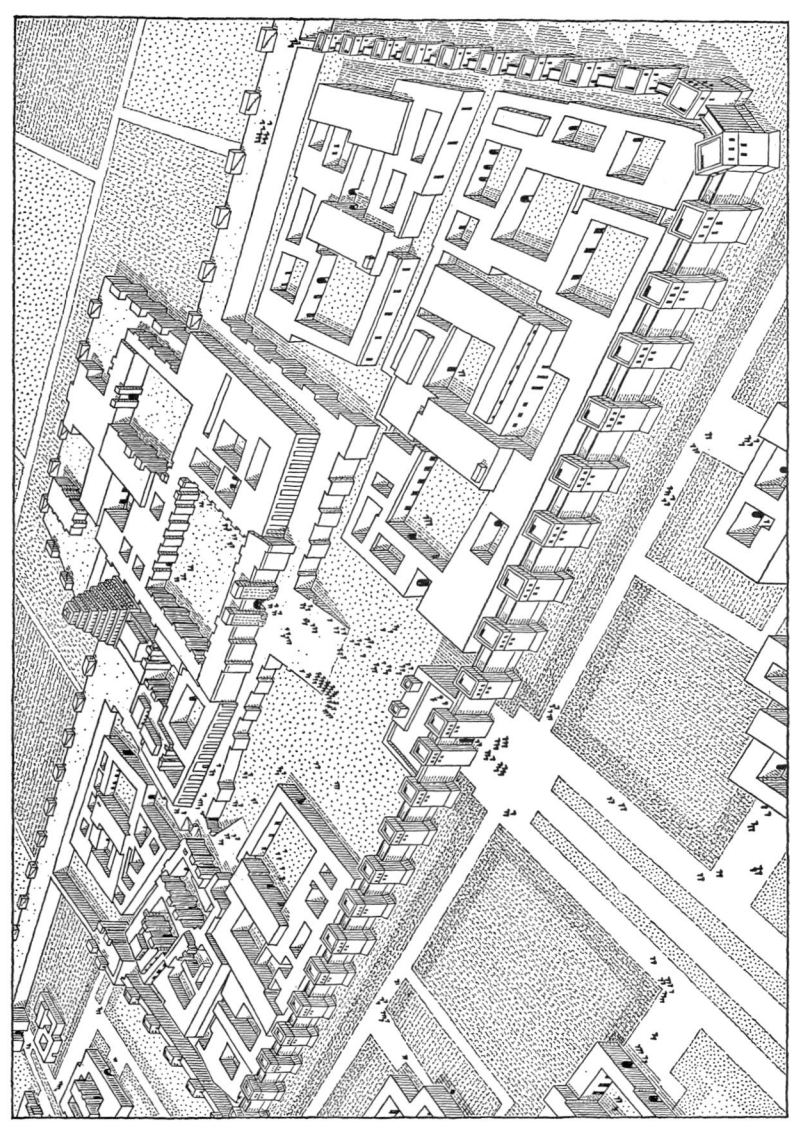

*Dur Sharrukin, Sargon's palace, 8th century* B.C. (*Reconstruction after Parrot*)

# The Men Who Deciphered Cuneiform

In 1761, Carsten Niebuhr journeyed to Egypt, Syria, and Arabia in the service of his country, Denmark, and this expedition led him into "forbidden" territory. And it was only because Niebuhr spoke Arabic and could pass as an Arab that he escaped alive from the terrible conditions that he and his companions encountered.

This frightful experience did not deter him from visiting Mesopotamia and Persia four years later. He got as far as Persepolis, spent three weeks making sketches and collecting inscriptions, and was the first person to recognize that cuneiform had been used not only for one language but for several different ones. Others followed in his tracks, and many attempts were made to decipher these strange signs, of which nothing at all was known at that time, not even the direction in which they were written.

One of the decisive steps forward was taken by a young teacher in Göttingen, Georg Grotefend, who already knew several ancient languages and had studied all the available texts from the Near East that he could lay his hands on. He was so eager to break the code that he actually laid a wager that he would decipher cuneiform, and, improbable as this sounds, he did in fact do so. With unique intuition, Grotefend deciphered some of the names of kings from a text in Old Persian, and he even identified the signs that divided the text into words. Thus the foundations for research were laid. A French scholar named

Burnouf and one of mixed German-Norwegian origin, Lasser, working informally in partnership, were able to isolate most of the cuneiform signs used in Old Persian, which was one of the languages under consideration.

Then Henry Creswicke Rawlinson came into the picture. As a schoolboy, it was the Greek and Latin historians who had interested him most of all, but when he was sent to India at the age of seventeen, he learned Hindustani, Persian, and Arabic, and soon became an interpreter. He was a fine horseman and he had no difficulty in getting along with the natives. On one journey to Persia in 1835, he observed a number of inscriptions carved on the cliffs of the Alwend Mountains. They were called "The Treasure Book" by the local people, and Rawlinson made copies of these inscriptions. Then one day he learned that there were other inscriptions of an enormous size engraved in the rocks of Behistun. He set off at once on horseback to see them. Behistun means "The Place of the Gods." On the southern side, there is a sacred mountain with twin peaks and a smooth wall of rock that falls sheer to the ancient highway linking Babylon and Ecbatana.

It was here that a Persian king, Darius I, had a vast monument chiseled in stone to commemorate his victory over his enemies "The Kings of Lies"—a record in words and pictures three hundred feet above the valley bottom. This victory is described in three languages, Old Persian, Elamite, and Babylonian. But no one knew that when Rawlinson appeared on the scene.

Several times a day Rawlinson scrambled up the precipice to the niches where the inscriptions stood. Working without any safety equipment was so laborious that errors were bound to creep into the copying. But twelve years later, Rawlinson returned to Behistun, and this time he had ropes and planks to help bridge the deep cleft which made access to the inscriptions themselves so difficult. Even then, a single false step might have meant his death.

The ledge of rock on which Rawlinson placed his ladders in order to reach the upper portion of the inscription is hardly two feet wide. A ladder long enough to reach the upper edge of the rock, would have had to be placed at such an acute angle that it would not carry a man. Therefore Rawlinson had to make do with a shorter ladder and risk his life by standing on the top rung. He could only contrive to keep his balance by supporting his body against his left arm, holding his notebook in his left hand and the pencil in his right. In this precarious position, he copied the entire upper portion which was in Old Persian. He was so absorbed in his task that he forgot all about the danger.

It proved even more difficult to approach the Elamite version of the text. Rawlinson tried to bridge the gap between the rocks with a ladder. This ladder had uprights of different lengths and only the longer of the two would just reach from one edge of the cleft to the other. Rawlinson laid the ladder across the gap. Grasping the upper shaft of wood with both hands to support himself, and with his feet resting on the lower bar, he began to cross the chasm. He was half way across when the lower shaft, which had been badly secured, went crashing down into the abyss. Rawlinson held on and proceeded hand over hand until he reached the other side.

There still remained the Old Babylonian portion to be copied. It had been carved in a place that was said to be quite inaccessible, even to the mountain folk, who were used to following the tracks of mountain goats without any effort. Rawlinson tried to read off the signs with the help of a telescope, but the result was inaccurate.

At length [wrote Rawlinson], a wild Kurdish boy . . . volunteered to make the attempt and I promised him a considerable reward if he succeeded. The mass of rock in question is scarped . . . so that it cannot be approached by any of the ordinary means of climbing. The boy's first move was to squeeze himself up a cleft in the rock a short distance to the left of the projecting mass. When he had ascended some distance above it, he drove a wooden peg firmly into the cleft, fastened a rope to this, and

then endeavored to swing himself across to another cleft at some distance on the other side; but in this he failed, owing to the projection of the rock. It then only remained for him to cross over the cleft by hanging on by his toes and fingers to the slight inequalities on the bare face of the precipice, and in this he succeeded, passing over a distance of twenty feet of almost smooth perpendicular rock in a manner which to a looker-on appeared quite miraculous. When he reached the second cleft, the real difficulties were over. He had brought a rope with him attached to the first peg, and now, driving in a second, he was able to swing himself right over the projecting mass of rock. Here with a short ladder he formed a swinging seat, like a painter's cradle, and, fixed upon this seat, he took under my direction the paper cast of the Babylonian translation of the records of Darius.

That was how, in the year 1847, the three texts were obtained, texts that repeated the same proclamation in three different languages. For the decipherment of cuneiform, they were as important as was the Rosetta Stone to Champollion, in his effort to throw a light on the obscurity of Egyptian hieroglyphics.

The Behistun monument closes with these words:

Thus says the King Darayavaush [Darius]: "Thou who, in days to come, seest this inscription which, at my command, has been struck in the rock, together with pictures of my men, do not deface it, do not destroy anything of it, take pains as long as life is in thee, to preserve it perfectly."

Rawlinson had done more. He had succeeded in wresting it from oblivion for all time. He dedicated several decades of his life to working at the decipherment of cuneiform, and more than once he was on the point of giving up. As more and more texts were discovered, the number of unknown signs grew to over five hundred. Scholars in various lands applied themselves to the laborious project. In 1851 Rawlinson published his bewildering

*Above and below: Dur Sharrukin (Khorsabad)*

Tall beaker from Susa
(beginning of 4th millenium B.C.)
(Paris)

conclusion that almost every cuneiform sign could stand for various different syllables. The experts were regarded with suspicion from all sides, and their disclosures were greeted with universal scepticism, even derision.

Then tablets were discovered in Nineveh which were virtually pages of dictionaries. This was a find no one had even dared to dream of. Opposite the Babylonian-Assyrian words stood the corresponding ones in Sumerian. It was a significant contribution and it led to final success. In order to prove that the decipherment of cuneiform had now been positively achieved in its essentials, four scholars, Rawlinson among them, were invited to make independent translations of a newly discovered text. They sent their translations to the Royal Asiatic Society in London in sealed envelopes, and at a solemn session the four covers were opened. When it was seen that the four versions corresponded in all the important points, the case was proved. That was in the year 1857.

It was about this time that a seventeen-year-old copperplate and banknote engraver named George Smith was working in

London. His work was so skillful that he was chosen to prepare the engravings of the tablets to illustrate Rawlinson's book on Assyrian cuneiform. Smith came from a humble home, and his parents could not afford to give him more than a few years' schooling. But on his own initiative, he had studied the Bible and all the books about the Near East he could lay his hands on. He spent so many hours in the British Museum that he attracted Rawlinson's attention, and it was at the latter's suggestion that he was appointed to the Museum's staff at the age of twenty-one.

Smith's task was the tedious one, sorting out the fragments of tablets discovered by Layard and Rassam in the mound of Kuyunjik and sent to London in crates and baskets. He had to help piece them together, an undertaking that seemed virtually hopeless. But no one had sharper eyes than Smith. He missed nothing, fitting pieces together according to the subtle variations in color tones or noticing how jagged edges would dovetail. But he had another great gift and that helped him even more. In an astonishingly short time, he learned to read the cuneiform signs, so that he was able to match up text fragments that belonged together. He even found the description of an eclipse—in cuneiform!

One day, he was working on a tablet that was still incomplete. About fifteen lines were missing, according to Smith's estimate. This was not the usual inventory of goods, as were most of the inscriptions so far, nor was it a decree, a letter, or a building specification. It was a story, and it told of a great deluge that had descended upon mankind in order to wipe out the human race; and of one man who had been advised by a god to build an ark and so survive the flood, together with his family and animals of every kind; and who, when the flood waters began to subside, sent out a raven and a dove in order to find out if dry land had reappeared. In fact, Smith was reading an account of the Flood, written in cuneiform long before the Bible had come into being.

On December 3, 1872, he published his discovery in the form

of a lecture. In the audience were a number of scholars, Rawlinson among them. There was great excitement throughout the world, and the *Daily Telegraph* offered a considerable sum of money for an expedition to be sent out to Mesopotamia, under Smith's leadership, to find the missing piece from the Babylonian version of the Flood. Smith accepted the commission. On January 20, 1873, he set off from London and on March 2, at nine o'clock in the morning, for the first time in his life he trod the ground where Nineveh had stood. Smith visited several sites in order to train his powers of observation.

On May 7, he began his excavation in the hill of Kuyunjik near the southwest palace of Sennacherib in which most of the archives from the Ashurbanipal library had been found. Several trenches were also dug in the northern palace of Ashurbanipal, but at first, little of importance came to light. The original excavators had left everything in an unholy mess, and in the intervening years the Arabs had used the site as a quarry. Blocks of stone had been carted away to build a bridge in Mosul.

At last fragments of inscribed tablets began to appear. On May 14, exactly one week after the excavation had begun, Smith was working on the day's finds, brushing the tablets to remove the earth that was still clinging to them. As he began to read one tablet of seventeen lines, he suddenly caught his breath. He held in his hand what he had set out to find. There were literally hundreds of thousands of broken splinters of clay buried in that vast rubbish heap, and his extraordinary luck—"excavator's luck"—had allowed him to light upon the one piece that contained the missing introduction to the story of the Flood that he was looking for. The complete cuneiform account of one of the greatest events of prehistoric times had now been rescued and Smith could read it:

At the time when Utnapishtim was king in the old city of Shuruppak, the gods burned with anger against mankind. Enlil advised the gods in council that they should send a great flood

*Bluebird fresco, Mari, 18th century* B.C. *(Paris)*

to drown the human race and the gods agreed to this, promising that none of them would betray the terrible secret to any human being. But Enki, the god of the watery deeps, did not want the race of man to perish and he whispered to the reed hut where Utnapishtim lived: "Reed hut, hear me. A great flood is coming soon and Utnapishtim would be well advised to build himself a great ark and to go inside it with all his family, taking animals of every kind and leaving all his wealth behind . . ."

Utnapishtim understood Enki's words and he built a great ark, and made it watertight with bitumen. He stocked it with oil, meat, and flour, and also with wine to celebrate the Feast of the New Year. And he led his family and animals of every species inside the ark and he locked the door from within. On the following day, black clouds covered the vault of the sky. The gods beat against the sluice gates of heaven until they broke. The earth grew livid beneath the terrible flashes of lightning and the ground splintered as a pot is shattered. The gods themselves grew afraid and slunk behind the clouds like dogs. Inanna, the goddess of love, screamed like a woman in travail: "Would that the day we decided to destroy mankind were turned to mud. My beloved people now fill the sea. It is choked with bodies as with fishspawn."

For six days and seven nights the south wind raged and the deluge did not cease. It was only on the seventh day that silence returned to the earth. Utnapishtim opened a hatch in the roof of the ark and light fell upon his countenance. And he saw an island, the peak of Mount Nisir. The mountain held the ark fast and for seven days, it would not let it sail away. Then Utnapishtim sent out a dove. The bird flew off and came back again, for it could find no place to rest. Next Utnapishtim sent out a swallow, and it too flew away only to return again, for it could find no resting place. Then Utnapishtim released a raven, and the raven did not return. It saw a place where the waters had subsided and there it perched, ate carrion, cawed, and let its droppings fall.

So Utnapishtim and his family left the ark and made a sacrifice to the gods, who gathered like flies round the offering, drawn thither by the sweet savor of the sacrifice. Only one god was angry, and that was Enlil. "There should have been no survivors," he declared. But Enki answered him: "You are too clever by half. You were too rash when you planned the total destruction of mankind. Let lions and wolves ravage them to keep their numbers down, for men are sinners. Let famine beset them. But there is one secret of the gods: They need men."

Then Enlil was won over. He stepped before Utnapishtim to thank him and he said: "Utnapishtim was a child of man and destined to die. Now he shall be safe from death, immortal like us gods." And the man through whom the human race was

*The Ishtar Gate, Babylon, at the time of Nebuchadnezzar II
(Reconstruction after Koldewey)*

preserved was given an island at the mouth of the rivers to be his dwelling place for all time.

This was the story that was written on the clay tablets, complete now after Smith's find. He announced his discovery in a cable to London and the news left everyone thunderstruck. Smith believed that his success would move the newspaper proprietors to even greater generosity, but in this he was mistaken. When he received a copy of the *Daily Telegraph* of May 21, 1873, he saw to his horror that his report had had a concluding sentence added to it: "This brings the excavation to an end."

There was nothing for Smith to do but return to London, although he nearly arrived empty-handed. The very idea of bribery shocked him, and he did not know much about oriental practices. So it was touch and go whether or not the Turkish customs officials would allow him to take with him the crates containing all his finds, or if they would confiscate them summarily. This time, however, all went well and back in England, Smith was able to obtain a fresh commission from the British Museum. The beginnings of 1874 saw him in Nineveh once more, and here he found the best part of another three thousand texts. But half of these were eventually confiscated because he still did not understand that the local pasha had financial worries which he expected the Englishman to relieve.

Two years later, Smith obtained a third excavation permit. On the way to Babylon he bought several thousand tablets from dealers in antiquities who had acquired them for next to nothing from grave robbers. It was high summer before he began the dig, and the workmen went on strike. They considered that such heavy work under the August sun was sheer lunacy. Smith fell ill and a caravan had to carry him to Aleppo, a physical wreck. There he died on August 19, 1876, at the age of thirty-six.

In the short time he was granted for his work, Smith made a decisive contribution to the task of restoring these long-buried civilizations. The story of the Flood brought the Land of Sumer to life again, for Shuruppak was a Sumerian city. The earliest history of the Land of the Two Rivers began to emerge in firm outline, and what that country had looked like five thousand years ago became clearer and clearer. Records like the story of the Flood pointed back to a time when the gods first created mankind and set them upon the face of the earth to be their heirs.

# Gods in the Land of Ur

Ashurbanipal, in whose library ruins Smith had found the missing piece of the story of the Flood, was the last of the great kings of Assyria. Very soon after his death, the kingdom he had led to a last burst of prosperity was destroyed. The Medes conquered Nineveh and the other Assyrian cities and razed them to the ground. The inhabitants were either slaughtered or enslaved. The Medes took a terrible revenge for the crimes that the Assyrians had committed against all their neighbors. The last Assyrian king threw himself into the flames at the fall of Nineveh, and since he had been a weak ruler, this act lived on in folk memory as Ashurbanipal's last deed.

Although Ashurbanipal was much feared by his enemies, it is he, more than any other king in the Land of the Two Rivers, who is responsible for preserving records from earlier millennia. The twenty-five thousand clay tablets that Layard and Rassam sent to London and were pieced together by Smith and others with such painstaking care, are probably only a small portion of the royal archives collected by Ashurbanipal at Nineveh. This monarch, unlike his predecessors, could read and write. On one tablet he reports with pride:

The god of scribes has bestowed on me the gift of the knowledge of his art. I have been initiated into the secrets of writing; I know the signs for heaven and earth and have taken up the word in the assembly of the masters. And just as I can ride fiery steeds, drive chariots, and forge weapons, so I can solve problems in calculation that are difficult to grasp. I can even read the intricate tablets in Sumerian, and I understand the enigmatic words in the stone engravings from the days before the Flood.

Ashurbanipal had many excellent scribes in his service. They used tablets of clay carefully prepared beforehand and they inscribed their texts under the guidance of scholars in particularly clear and beautifully written signs. They recorded Sumerian texts side by side with their translation into Akkadian, the language which the king normally used. The inscribed tablets were kiln-fired, and that explains why they were able to survive the destruction of Nineveh and the long journey from the Tigris to the Thames, although not without some damage. On them were preserved laws and decrees, catalogs and prescriptions, incantations and prayers, proverbs and fables, hymns and epics.

Ashurbanipal was a passionate collector. His tentacles reached out far beyond the frontiers of Assyria. When he had conquered Babylon, he had many tablets from the libraries of Babylonian temples brought to Nineveh. Commands like this were sent out north, south, east, and west.

Word of the king to Shadunu: It is well with me; may you be happy. When you receive this letter, take with you the learned men of the city of Borsippa, and seek out all the tablets, all those that are in their houses, and all those that are deposited in the temple. . . . Hunt for the valuable tablets which are in your archives and which do not exist in Syria and send them to me. I have written to the officials and overseers . . . and no one shall withhold a tablet from you, and when you see any tablet . . . which . . . may be profitable for my palace, seek it out, pick it up, and send it to me.

And that is how such a wealth of documents was collected for Ashurbanipal's library.

The *tell* in which the remains of the Sumerian city of Nippur lay hidden turned out to be a most important source of written tablets. An American archaeological expedition dug there between 1888 and 1900. During the first winter of the dig much time was wasted, for the leader of the expedition quarreled with the finest scholar in his team, the Assyriologist H. V. Hilprecht. In spite of this, however, a test dig at a spot suggested by Hilprecht brought two thousand tablets to light, and in the third season, there were five thousand. On the final dig, led by Hilprecht himself with admirably clear-sighted vision, more than seventeen thousand texts were dug out of the so-called Hill of Tablets. Of these texts, there are more than two thousand examples of hymns and stories from the earliest times. In 1923 Arno Poebel published a grammar of the Sumerian language. A number of scholars, headed first and foremost by Professor S. N. Kramer, labored for many decades with the translations of these texts, some of which had been written more than four thousand years ago. Kramer alone was able to reconstruct to a considerable extent nine Sumerian epics and fourteen tales of the gods that go back to the earliest versions, as well as innumerable short passages of various kinds. And so the story of Sumer can be told from the very beginning. We now know about their first kings, whom they worshiped as gods, although their very names had disappeared from the face of the earth for more than two thousand years.

Lord of the earth was the ruler of the gods, Enlil. He was the one who had advised the council of the gods to annihilate the human race, and who later granted eternal life to Utnapishtim. It was Enlil who carried out the decisions taken in the council of the gods. His voice called up the hurricane of destruction that came as a punishment when the divine order was disturbed. Enlil also used hostile armies sometimes to punish the disobedient. As one ancient tablet reads:

Enlil summons the storm; the people lament. He takes away the refreshing wind from the land; the people lament. The wind that makes man rejoice he removes from the Land of Sumer

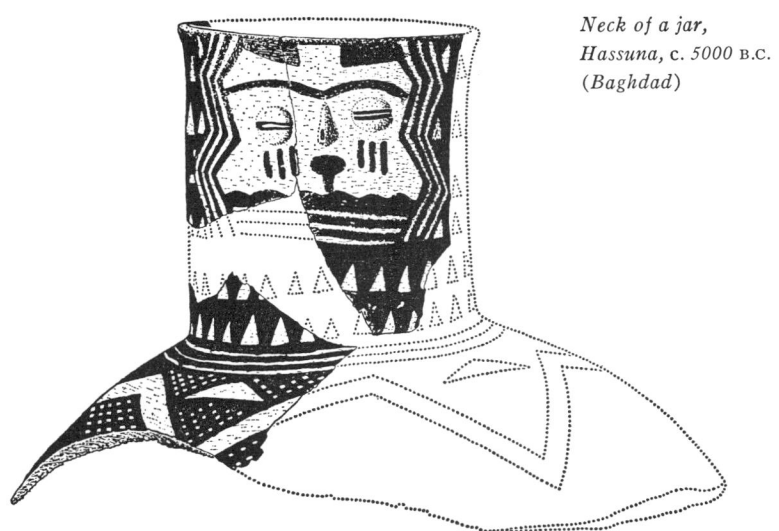

*Neck of a jar, Hassuna, c. 5000 B.C. (Baghdad)*

and he sends the devastating tempest. He summons the storm that destroys; the people lament. He sends the gale that lays waste, the thunderstorm that engulfs the ships like a tidal wave; the people lament. He fans the flame of the raging wind, the scorching breath of the desert. With the hurricane that destroys everything in its path, he covers the land as with a black cloth. And the city falls in ruins, the narrow lanes and the streets are littered with corpses like splinters of broken pots. Gates and walls gape wide; the dead lie in the squares and the fields, and the blood of the land fills the ditches as molten brass fills a mold.

But Enlil was not only a god of judgment and retribution. He encouraged the earth to blossom and bear fruit. His breath turned the desert green after the rains. At his command the sheep dropped their lambs, the goats their kids, and in the good fields of Sumer the corn raised its golden head. But he was not a benevolent god.

The assembly of the gods was presided over by Anu who ruled the skies. Anu's duty was to prevent unholy discord from breaking out among the gods. The word for argument in Sumerian means literally "to question one another." This held good for the gods, too. And only when everyone had had his say did Anu speak: "So be it!" and the decision of the gods was put into effect.

The largest shrine to Anu was built in Uruk. But neither Uruk nor Nippur, where Enlil reigned, were numbered among the oldest cities, at least according to the story of the Flood. Here, five towns are mentioned by name: Shuruppak, which was the place where Utnapishtim lived, Sippar, Larak, Badtibira, and Eridu. In each of these cities a god had been enthroned as the first king.

Eridu, which the Sumerians themselves thought of as their most ancient town, and which was, in their eyes, holier than all others, belonged to the water-god, Enki. Eridu was built near the sea in the south of the country, and it stood by a lagoon, where the seawater mingled with the sweet water of the rivers. Enki, "lord of the watery deeps," had stepped ashore at this spot, and when he looked up, he saw the great constellations moving across the sky like oxen, and the small stars scattered round the moon like grains of corn.

Enki was the god of wisdom, whose heart was unfathomable. He blessed the trees and the reeds, birds and men; he invented the plough and the pick, the molds to shape bricks, he framed laws and decrees. In his travels across the world, he visited the other gods and ordained the fates of the various countries. He created healing herbs, he gave the winds their orders, and he taught mankind how to construct canals that would serve both for irrigation and drainage. Then he returned to Eridu. And as he was the god who possessed all the divine powers that benefit the human race, Enki's divine home on earth was especially revered. It was to his city that the people of Sumer gave pre-eminence.

Anu, the god of Uruk, saw this and was envious. He conferred with his daughter Inanna, with whom he shared the dominion of Uruk. And she sailed down the river to the city of Eridu to pay Enki a visit. Enki gave a banquet in her honor. At the feast he grew merry and he drank so much that he no longer knew what he was doing. Inanna so bewitched him with her loveliness that when she asked him to give her all the divine laws and powers, he made her a present of them. The craft of building; the skills of the tanner, the basketmaker, the smith, and the carpenter; the arts of reading and calculating as well as the design of musical instruments and equipment to observe the stars—all human knowledge and all skills he presented to Inanna.

In great haste, Inanna heaped the precious gifts into her bark and set off for Uruk. It was too late when Enki recovered from his drunken stupor. When he realized the harm he had done himself, he sent a messenger and a horde of sea monsters after Inanna to confiscate the bark and all the gifts that were in it. The messenger overtook Inanna and addressed her with these words: "Oh, my queen, Enki sends me to you. The words of the master of the deep are sublime, you may not cast them to the winds. He orders you to hand over the bark with all its cargo and to continue your journey to Uruk on foot." Then Inanna spoke. "Why has Enki changed his mind? Why does he break his word of honor and bring disgrace on his solemn promise?"

When the sea monsters heard these words, they laid hold of the boat, but Inanna resisted their attack with the help of her retinue, and the monsters had to return to Eridu, their mission unaccomplished. Seven times more did Enki send them back to the goddess, but each time she won the battle for the bark. Safe and sound, she landed back in Uruk and, amidst the jubilation of the people, she unloaded the priceless freight. Now Inanna became the goddess of skills in the city of the god of the skies, Anu.

Inanna always wanted to have her own way. It was against her father's wishes that she declared war on the god of the northern mountains. And it was against his advice that she married the shepherd-king Dumuzi, for Anu wanted Enkimdu, the god of farmers, to be her husband. The two wooers had a fierce dispute in which each poured scorn on the other's qualities, but afterward they became good friends. Dumuzi invited Enkimdu to the wedding feast, and later he was allowed to pasture his beasts in Enkimdu's fields. Inanna knew very well that both were necessary for the Land of Sumer—the man who tilled the soil and dug the canals, as well as the keeper of livestock.

It was thanks to Inanna that Dumuzi was enthroned as king of Uruk, and because it was her doing, she felt herself all-powerful. Dominion over the earth no longer satisfied her. She wanted to rule the underworld too, which was the domain of her older sister, Ereshkigal. Inanna tied the divine laws to her girdle, placed the crown of the plains on her head, took a measuring rod of lapis lazuli in her right hand, placed a golden ring on her left hand, and bound a shield of stone to her breast. Then she descended into the kingdom of the dead in order to conquer her sister, saying to her chancellor: "If I have not returned to Uruk after three days and three nights, then go to the other gods, so that one of them may come to my aid."

Boldly Inanna entered her sister's kingdom, which was guarded by seven gates. Pale with wrath, Ereshkigal spoke to the keeper of the gates. "Fling open the gates so that Inanna may enter. But she shall come into my presence bowing low, stripped and naked shall she appear before me."

And the keeper of the gates threw them open. At the first gate, the divine laws were taken away from Inanna, at the second gate, the crown of the plains. At each gate, yet another possession was removed from her until she stood at last, defenseless, before Ereshkigal, her sister and enemy. And Ereshkigal turned the eye of death on Inanna and spoke the word of doom. At once Inanna stiffened into a corpse. In vain did the people of Uruk wait for her return, but it never occurred to Dumuzi to go

*The Ishtar Gate, Babylon (Berlin)*
*Following pages: "The Dairy Frieze," Al Ubaid, 3rd millenium* B.C. *(Baghdad)*

to Inanna's rescue. On the fourth day, therefore, the chancellor went to Nippur and begged Enlil to go and help Inanna. Enlil refused. The chancellor then went to Ur, to the god of the moon. The moon-god refused, too. At last the chancellor went to Eridu. And Enki listened to him, although Inanna had won the laws of the gods from him by a trick. He sent two messengers into the underworld, and they took with them the bread of life and the water of life.

They crumbled the bread over Inanna and sprinkled her with the water so that she was restored to life, and Ereshkigal had to release her sister from the kingdom of the dead. But it was understood that someone else had now to leave the land of the living in her place, for such was the law. When Dumuzi was chosen in exchange and confronted by the revived queen and the ruthless ambassadors of Ereshkigal, he refused to lie down in the dust and die. So demons seized him by force and carried him off to the underworld.

In the council of the gods, however, it was decided that Dumuzi would be allowed to return to life every year, to celebrate anew his marriage to Inanna so that the Land of Sumer would be fertile and not become a wilderness again. Ereshkigal, the goddess of death, agreed. She wanted to rule over as many dead as she possibly could. But as people had to be born before they could die, it was in her interests to send Dumuzi back to earth as the bringer of new life. Just as morning after morning, the sun-god Utu breaks out of his prison, the Mountains of the Night, so Dumuzi would return to Uruk after every winter of death, to the city where stood the House of Heaven, the temple of E-anna.

The walls of this shrine were found in the rubbish mound of Warka by German archaeologists during the winter of 1929–30. They dug down to a considerable depth before the foundations of limestone slabs appeared. The temple was about two hundred and sixty feet long and ninety-nine feet wide and many important finds were made within its precincts.

Bull-god and goddess, Susa, 2nd millenium B.C. (Paris)

On February 22, 1939, the workmen who were employed on the excavation suddenly began to dance and sing for joy, a sure sign that they had come upon a considerable discovery. The leader of the expedition, Heinz Lenzen, hurried to the spot. A marble head lay face down among the remains of an old building that had been constructed of narrow sun-baked bricks, known as *Riemchen* bricks. With the utmost care, Lenzen eased away the marble head from the surrounding earth. It was a woman's face that was brought into the light once more, after thousands of years in darkness. Cut as it was from clear, almost translucent marble, it seemed to be alive. The nose was partly destroyed, the eyes and eyebrows were missing, as well as the wig—or helmet—that must once have covered the head. But mouth, cheeks, chin, and forehead were undamaged and the empty eye sockets gazed out as if from another world.

This marble head of Uruk found on that February day dates from an age from which only a few statues representing men or gods have survived. It is likely that it was an image of the mighty goddess who went down into the underworld and was held prisoner there for three days.

Another sensational discovery was made in the E-anna temple —an alabaster vase, over three feet in height. It was lying in fifteen pieces when the team found it, and it had been bound with copper bands. This showed that the vase had been broken once before and repaired again, a sign of the importance attached to it in Sumerian times.

There are four rows of decoration running round the vase. At the bottom there are plants rising from the water, the element of life. The second row depicts rams and ewes. Above this is a procession of men carrying the harvest's first fruits and sacrificial animals to the temple, before which stands the goddess Inanna awaiting them. The two bundles of reeds that rise behind her like pillars are the symbols of her divinity. Unfortunately there is little left of the figure of the king but his mesh skirt and the train borne by a servant, but he is leading

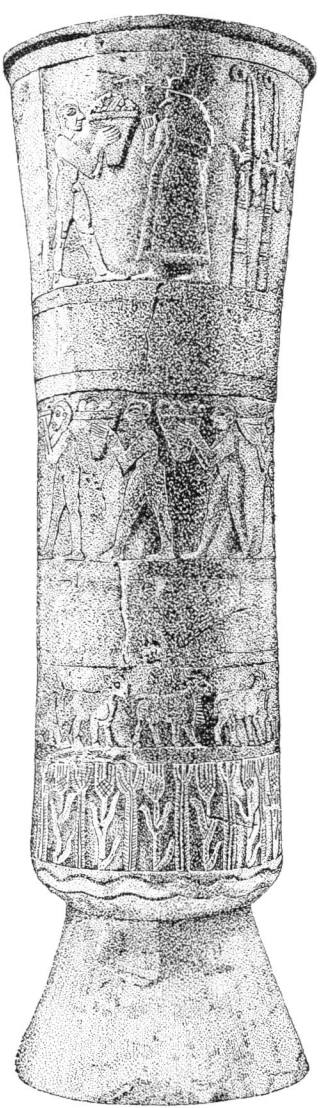

*Alabaster vase, Uruk, early 3rd millenium* B.C. (*Baghdad*)

the bringers of gifts who advance to sacrifice the finest produce in the land to Inanna. The food will be stored inside the temple.

It was by these sacrifices in the temples that men kept the gods alive. That was why they were created. This story is told in one of the oldest myths found so far:

At the beginning of time there were only gods on earth, and they had to break their backs, wresting their sustenance from the soil. The gods dug out the canals and dredged them year after year. They sweated and strained with plough and pick, they cultivated the fields and they harvested with sickles. Such hard toil was repugnant to them and they held a council of the gods to discuss it. Enki, the wise, whom they awakened from a deep slumber, proposed that they should create human beings to serve them, so that the gods could give more time to their divine duties. And Enki himself took clay that rose from the depths of the sea. With this clay he shaped human beings and he breathed life into them, but only enough for them to live a human span. As a form of tribute for their creation, however, they were obliged to keep the tables of the gods supplied with food and drink. And the gods gave to men the land between the two rivers. "Make it into a paradise," the gods demanded. And so men set themselves to work.

So it says in the cuneiform signs written on tablets of clay. But the story of the beginnings of civilization in the Land of the Two Rivers is told in other ways besides words.

The days when explorers were content to come across lucky finds by chance are long since past. For half a century now the work has been done scientifically, the earth has been carefully removed, stratum by stratum, right down to the base of alluvial soil originally deposited by the Tigris and Euphrates. In many places, it was necessary to dig over eighty feet deep before reaching virgin soil, that is, until no trace of human activity could be detected. In the lower layers, the excavators found tools and vessels from 5000 B.C. Professional archaeologists can tell immediately which period their finds belong to, for the fragments disclose their age by their shape, color, and decoration. Copper tools are older than iron ones, stone ones are older than copper. When man first arrived in the Land of the Two Rivers, he did not know yet how to fashion metals. But he soon learned.

# The Creation of Paradise

Five thousand years ago, the Euphrates flowed many miles farther east than it does today and the Tigris, too, has changed its riverbed in the course of time. From the beginning of time, these two rivers were unpredictable in their behavior. Their old course is indicated by the mounds in which the lost cities of the Sumerians and Babylonians have been discovered. When these cities were still inhabited, the sea came several hundred miles farther inland than it does today, and the mouths of the Tigris and the Euphrates were some distance apart.

Seven thousand years ago no cities had yet been established in the Land between the Two Rivers. Every year the low-lying plains were inundated and became huge lakes, and when the water subsided great swamps remained behind, one vast stretch of uninhabited wasteland. In the summer, the swamps dried out. Thunderstorms gathered over the plains, drenching them in vivid green as the lightning played over them. This was a land that offered no security for habitation.

Men dared not linger long in territory that was so subject to flooding. They wandered along the upland valleys and the steppes, and there they got what they needed for their existence by hunting. The arrow with which they killed their prey assured them their vital food. (Thousands of years later, the Sumerians used one sign to denote both "life" and "arrow"—*ti*.)

But gradually the steppes dried out. The wild game migrated and the hunters began to domesticate animals and become shepherds. They collected fruits and started tilling fields. They cast greedy eyes on the marshland where the reeds stood man-high. And they ventured to extend their fields down to the edge of the land that was subject to flooding, for the soil there was many times more fertile than higher up. But the rivers were treacherous. In one year they carried down too little water, in another, too much. Sometimes the ground was too dry, sometimes too wet. The farmers began to dig ditches and bank the sides of streams, to control the amount of water that reached the fields. When they had proved to their own satisfaction that they could get the better of the water by means of ditches and embankments, the settlers became bolder; they penetrated more deeply into the clumps of reeds and they drained more and more swamps. By means of rills, streams, and rivers they themselves had created, they reduced the violence of the waters and diverted their courses. Irrigation channels meant that moisture and fertile mud were carried to places where formerly a pitiless sun had scorched the earth. Men tamed the rivers and the land was theirs. The plains were turned into an enormous cultivated field that yielded rich harvests every year.

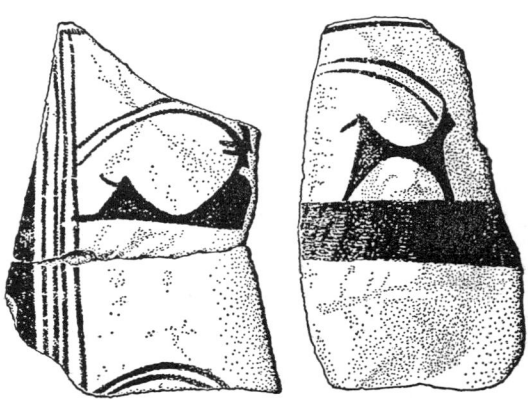

*Painted pottery fragments, Telloh, 4th millenium* B.C. *(Paris)*

The population increased, the villages quickly grew in size. At first the people were satisfied to live in huts made of reeds. Then they took pieces of clay and shaped them into lumps and built mud huts. Later still, they learned to form bricks and to bake them in the sun. The houses became more and more capable of withstanding the elements, even the storms could no longer harm them. Their implements, weapons, and pottery improved steadily. They bartered copper for corn, as the old name for the Euphrates tells us, for the earliest settlers called it Urutu, the Copper River. The copper came from the mountains in the north. With metal weapons and tools, it was easier for them both to ward off danger and to accomplish their daily tasks.

The settlers learned to survive. They clung to life so strongly that they could not believe that death meant the end of everything. If a member of a family died, he still kept his place in the home and was buried in the ground on which the house stood. And as the dead had everything that a living person needs on hand, the corpse was not buried with either weapons or vessels. The family meals were shared between the living and the dead.

Instead of the simple red, gray, and black pottery, gradually there developed painted bowls and jars which became more and more beautiful. Patterns incorporated birds with fish in their beaks, people with flowing hair, or goats with massive horns, and these designs reveals both great craftsmanship and also a strongly marked sense of order.

Order was a prime consideration for these people, for without it they could not have survived. The rivers were a constant threat. Many a spring they rose with such uncanny speed that the canals overflowed, the embankments were torn down, and the fields were ruined. So the inhabitants of several villages got together to build bigger canals. They chose one man from their midst as their prince and they called him Lugal: Great Man. He was also high priest in the temple that was built to house the guardian god, and it was around these temples that the first towns developed.

*Central hall of the White Temple, Uruk
(Reconstruction after E. Heinrich)*

Excavations at Tell Halaf and other places have brought conclusive evidence that there were temples with niches in the walls and a system of irrigation in use in the Land of the Two Rivers as early as approximately 4000 B.C. The oldest settlements include those of Al Ubaid, Hassuna, Samarra, and Ka'lat Jarmo. Eridu is considered to be the oldest of the cities. Iraqi archaeologists who excavated there found fourteen temples built one on top of the other, all dating from before the Flood. In Warka, a German team discovered a stratum forty feet thick containing evidence of settlements from the third millennium. In the Land of the Two Rivers, there are several mounds known as the Hill of the Seven Cities and many of these *tells* conceal ruins of more than a mere seven towns. If you cross Iraq by air, not only can you pick out the network of canals that was constructed thousands of years ago but you can also see clearly the sites where the old cities stood.

The city centers were their temples, splendid buildings with several courtyards. These temples rose on terraces made of rough lumps of clay. The walls were built of mud bricks and the surface was plastered over with a layer of stucco. The mud was washed up by the rivers and it was along these rivers that the precious slabs of stone were transported to be used as cladding, sometimes for foundations, sometimes for walls. Often there were clay pegs as long as one's finger driven into the mud plaster. They had flat heads variously colored black, white, and red, and they made an artistic pattern on the wall, not unlike those one sees in woven matting. These pegs were also used to make brilliant mosaic decorations on pillars of mud brick, an adornment fit for the house of a god.

Every city had its own deity who looked after the well-being of the inhabitants. In his service were the farmers who tilled the fields, the men who dredged the canals to keep them clear of mud, the shepherds, the craftsman—everyone, including the Lugal, acted in the service of the god.

The Lugal was both the highest servant of the god and his representative as well. The princess, similarly, was the high priestess of the god's consort. The prince's children were the special servants of the children of the god. In addition, there were numerous temple officials. A keeper of the gate had to guard the entrance to the holy of holies. One man saw to it that the food was correctly prepared, another supervised the temple breweries. The god had his armorers, heralds, bodyguards, charioteers, cattlemen, and storekeepers. There was even a special goatherd to supply milk and cheese for the god's family. Temple musicians gladdened the god's ear and a drummer beat the drum when the god was roused to anger. For the beating of the drum pacified the wrathful heart of the god.

The whole territory belonged to the god. The meadow bailiffs, the gamekeepers, the fishery superintendents, the watchers on the city walls all had to report to the temple at regular intervals, like every other employee. The Lugal received their reports and issued orders so that fields and fishponds, canals, walls, and workshops were all maintained in good order. He decided what payment was to be made for each service and he supervised the bookkeeping. He administered justice and protected the weak, all in the service of the god. Everything was so thoroughly steeped in the will of the god, that not only men but fields, rivers, winds, and stars were considered members of his community. In them too, was the spark of life, the breath of the wise god Enki. One could address one's words to any kind of object: "Flint, how hard and dark you are! Be kind and make sparks to give us fire! ... Salt, created in the pure place, give savor to our food! Mud, turn into brick!" And all these things obeyed.

Everything radiated from the temple precincts, the dwellings of the ruler of the city and of the priests, the workshops, granaries and schools, the living houses of the people, the streets and the squares.

The ranking of a city depended on the order which the city god held in the assembly of gods. Eridu was the holiest city, for it was the shrine of the god Enki, who had created mankind and given him his inventions, the pick and the plough, measuring rod and chisel, the arts and the sciences. Uruk, too, was held in high esteem, for it was there that Anu, the god of the skies, had his shrine. Inanna, his daughter, had brought the laws of the god to Uruk and it was there that she had married Dumuzi, the divine shepherd, and raised him to be king. Dominion over the whole of Sumer was associated with the city of Nippur. Here ruled Enlil, "king of all the lands," who made the day dawn, who designed the city plans, and who looked after the growth, welfare, and prosperity of the land of Sumer.

Among the tablets found by the American excavation team in Nippur were many inscribed with hymns of praise to the reigning deity, Enlil. Here is a free rendering of one of these poems:

Enlil is the lord whose command is far-reaching, who forever decrees destinies. His eye scans the lands and searches the heart of Sumer. He does not tolerate the arrogant or the oppressor in

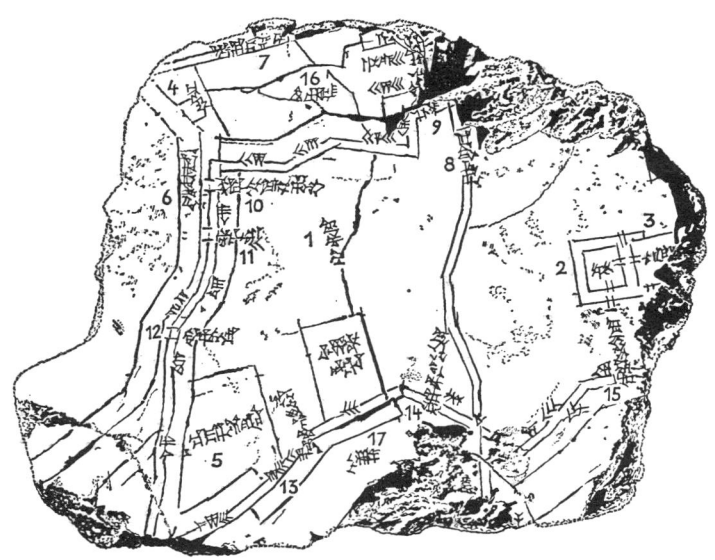

*Clay tablet showing the town plan of Nippur (about 1500 B.C.), probably the oldest town plan in the world. The inscriptions are mainly in Sumerian. Key: 1. Name of town EN-LIL-KI; 2. Ekur (Temple); 3. Kiur (Temple); 4. Eshmah ("The exalted shrine"); 5. Kirishauri (Town park or gardens); 6. Euphrates; 7. Canal; 8. Idshauri ("City-center canal"); 9–15. Gates; 16–17. City walls with moats; (After S. N. Kramer, Hilprecht Collection, Jena)*

his city, Nippur. He holds the great net in his hand, and the wicked and the evildoer cannot escape from its meshes. He has established his dwelling on the throne of his temple. His laws are like the laws of the abyss, none can look upon them. Without Enlil, no cities would be built, no villages founded, no sheepfolds erected. Without Enlil, no king would be raised to the throne, no high priest born. Workers would have no supervisor to direct them. The rivers would not know when to rise in spate, the fish of the sea would not spawn, the birds of the sky would not build their nests. Without Enlil, the clouds would not give rain; flowers and herbs, the glory of the plain, would fail to grow. The fields would yield no harvest, the meadows would not be green with grass, the orchards would bear no fruit. Enlil, the sublime shepherd, is ever on the move. He is the king of all who draw breath. From him stems the kingship and he it is who places the crown on the king's head.

According to the beliefs of the Sumerians, the kingship descended twice from heaven to earth: first at the beginning of time and secondly after the great Flood.

In the days of Alexander the Great, a Babylonian priest named Berossos drew up in Greek the Sumerian "king-lists," and thus the names of individual kings and their dynasties were handed down to posterity, together with the lengths of their reigns. According to these lists, the ten most ancient kings before the Deluge were gods or the sons of gods. The tenth king was Utnapishtim of Shuruppak, to whom Enki revealed the dread secret of the gods and their intention to destroy mankind.

The first dynasty after the Flood had its royal palace in Kish, but later it was moved to Babylon. Twenty-three kings belonged to this dynasty, and their combined reigns were said to cover a period of twenty-four thousand years. They were followed by the first dynasty of Uruk, with twelve kings, and two thousand three hundred years of rulership were attributed to them. Then the kingship passed to the first dynasty of Ur, and the five kings of Ur reigned for one hundred and seventy-seven years.

To begin with, these old Mesopotamian king-lists were held to be purely mythical. The fabulous lengths of the reigns were taken literally, and if the figures had been used in our sense of numbers, they were clearly impossible. But what the chronicler was trying to convey was that these early kings were endowed with superhuman powers, and that what they accomplished would have needed centuries for ordinary human beings. Therefore, because of their exalted status and their mighty deeds, the years of their reigns were multiplied by ten or even by a hundred.

Even the archaeologists believed at first that the early kings in the king-lists were legendary. Then excavations in Ur and Al Ubaid nearby succeeded in throwing new light on prehistoric times. In the 1923–24 season, Sir Leonard Woolley found a golden bead in Al Ubaid engraved with a king's name, and this also appeared on a tablet. The king was called Aannepadda. And at the excavation of Ur, seals and seal impressions and splendid grave-gifts in gold, silver, and semiprecious stones were found that had belonged to kings. On one limestone slab stood the name Mesannepadda. He, however, was named in the king-lists as the founder of the first dynasty of Ur, and Aannepadda was mentioned as his son and successor. At one blow, heroes of romance were confirmed as historically verified sovereigns who had ruled from their palace in Ur and had received the crown in Nippur. The founder of the dynasty was especially revered as such, and he was, therefore, attributed with a reign lasting eighty years; for his successors there were reigns of between twenty-five and thirty-six years. We may take these latter figures at their face value.

The thirteenth king of the first dynasty of Kish was credited with a reign of no less than one thousand five hundred years. His name was Etana and he also carried a nickname, "the Shepherd." He accomplished great deeds and had the gods as his helpers and friends, which was nothing unusual in those far-off times.

His consort, the queen, could only bear her children in long travail and with great risk to her life, and the king was so deeply troubled when another child was due to be born that he went to the temple and asked Enlil what could be done. Enlil told Etana that the herb to bring about easy childbirth was reserved for the gods and was kept in heaven. The king was not discouraged by this answer. He had saved the young of the heavenly eagle by killing the snake that threatened their lives, and now Etana besought the eagle to carry him up to heaven. The eagle agreed and rose into the air with Etana on its back.

Etana looked down and saw towns and villages grow small.

*Etana's Flight to Heaven, cylinder seal, 3rd millenium B.C. (Berlin)*

The earth dwindled and shrank until at last it was no bigger than the palm of a man's hand. Then fear struck its talons into Etana's heart. He grew afraid that he would never find his way back to earth again if he rose any higher, and he clutched at the eagle's neck. In spite of its powerful wings the eagle could not rise higher and had to return to earth. Thus the herb of easy childbirth was denied to human beings. When the king entered the temple after his flight to heaven, he learned from Enlil that pain is part of the tribute that men must pay to the gods. Not only must mortals work for the immortals to whom they owe their existence, they must also suffer for them in order to fulfil the laws of the gods. And Etana had to bow his head and accept this destiny.

Another king, however, rebelled against it: the fifth king of the dynasty of Uruk. His name was Gilgamesh.

*Vessel from Khafajah, 4th millenium B.C. (Baghdad)*

# Gilgamesh Protests

The deeds of Gilgamesh lived for more than two thousand years in the folk memory of the Mesopotamian peoples and their neighbors. His mightiest achievement was the building of the walls around the city of Uruk. But when the excavators first found clay tablets which mentioned his name, when they read of his adventures and particularly when he was said to be two-thirds a god and one-third a man, they took it for granted that he was a mythical hero and not a real king.

Then one day positive evidence of the walls that Gilgamesh built appeared clearly marked in the desert sand. The team that had been digging in Uruk for several seasons could not believe their eyes. It was true that an Englishman, William Kennet Loftus, had discovered partial remains of walls there one hundred years before and had sketched them in on his maps. And during the excavations of 1912–13 an earlier German expedition had come upon portions of a perimeter wall concealed in a chain of hills. But now, in December 1934, such a wall was suddenly revealed in its entire length. The official report explains how it happened in these terms: It is known that on ruined sites the ground moisture is absorbed and released at varying rates (*e.g.* for brickwork, rubble, talus, and so on) depending on the amount of saltpeter they contain. Thanks to this fact, the whole course of the ancient city wall suddenly became visible to the naked eye. A phenomenon that occurs once in a hundred years had come to the aid of the expedition, and they had no difficulty in plotting

*Above and below: Calah, Nimrud*

the course of the broad ribbon that had unrolled itself in the sand so unexpectedly and recording it on the maps of Uruk. A few cross-sections were dug to confirm that the wall did indeed lie buried in the sand, and these gave ample evidence of the original structure.

Uruk had unveiled its greatest secret in a single night—the walls of Gilgamesh. They are more than eight miles long, and even now they are nearly twenty feet high in many places and fifteen feet thick. Every eleven to thirteen yards, there once stood a semicircular turret, and in all, there were more than nine hundred of such towers perched above the wall proper. It enclosed the whole city, with its temples and houses, the dwellings of the poor, burial grounds, gardens, and fields. There were only two gates in it, one in the north facing Nippur and Kish, and the other to the south leading to Ur and Eridu.

For the building of the wall, bricks of an unusual shape were used. They were rather like a loaf, flat below and slightly domed on top. The archaeologists knew that bricks like this were used in 2700 B.C. for building Mesopotamian temples, palaces, and fortifications, and thus they established that this was the period when Gilgamesh ruled in Uruk.

The construction of the wall must have kept the people of Uruk slaving away for decades. This, too, is confirmed in the records that have survived. Indeed, the great Gilgamesh epic opens with a lament over the severe hardship suffered by the people of Uruk through the building of the wall. When George Smith first discovered the account of the Flood, he had never even heard of Gilgamesh, the king who had a greater reputation than any other monarch of prehistoric times. Very soon, however, Smith deduced that it was Gilgamesh who had built the great wall of Uruk, and that it was to him that Utnapishtim had told the story of the catastrophic flood and how it had brought him immortality. Smith found references to Gilgamesh on more and more tablets in the collection at the British Museum.

At last he came upon one particular observation by a scribe

that informed him about the length of the epic. It must have consisted of some twelve tablets. Smith consulted British, French, and German scholars and a great search began for the parts still missing from the most important poem from the Land of the Two Rivers.

Smith himself made a start with two finds. When he learned from the newspaper report that his excavation was now at an end, he refused to stop digging as long as he had a penny left. The money lasted for another two weeks. In those last days, he found stone reliefs and painted tiles, and also half a clay tablet on which were written four vertical rows of cuneiform signs standing side by side. The first row showed the pronunciation of the words, the second the way they were usually written, the third was a transcription, and the fourth, the literal meaning. With the uncanny certainty of a sleepwalker that had already guided him to the missing fragment of the story of the Flood, Smith discovered the other half of the "dictionary" tablet embedded in the roof of a gallery that followed the course of a wall. The half tablet was easily prised out, and Smith did it so neatly that the reversed cuneiform inscription was preserved like mirror-writing in the roof of the gallery. He was further rewarded for his acute observation, for not far from this place, he found two more fragments of tablets from which he could decipher additional portions of the Gilgamesh epic. All the cuneiform experts set to work to tackle this poem, whose hero was not a god after all but a mortal man who had made a vigorous protest against the idea of dying.

Between 1911 and 1935, twenty-six Sumerian tablets and fragments containing bits of the Gilgamesh epic were scrutinized by scholars in England, France, Germany, and Turkey. And, since 1935, Professor Kramer has found over sixty more fragments among the extensive collections in Philadelphia and Istanbul which are now available, thanks to him. There is no doubt today that this epic is the earliest example of great literature known to us. Gilgamesh, the Sumerian king, was also a celebrated hero among the Babylonians and Assyrians, the Hurrians and the Hittites. In the final Babylonian version, the epic has some three thousand five hundred lines, and the meaning of about two thousand of these has been deciphered so far.

Here are the adventures and fate of the most famous king of Uruk:

Gilgamesh, son of the shepherd-god Dumuzi, grandson of the fisherman-god Lugalbanda, built a wall around his city to make it safe against attack. Its pinnacles shone like brass. Its outer surface was armored with stone cladding, every brick had been hardened in the fire. The people of Uruk groaned beneath the burden of the building of the wall, for Gilgamesh drove them on without pity. He was like the wild bull in strength, for he was two-thirds a god and one-third a man. The drums that summoned the people to work were sounded without a pause, so that the son had no time to spend with his father, nor the lover with his lady. And the people complained to Anu, the god of the skies, that Gilgamesh oppressed his people cruelly and there was no one as strong as he to challenge his tyranny. Thereupon Anu created a man as strong as Gilgamesh, the savage Enkidu. Enkidu's body was felted with matted hair, and his wild locks hung down as long as cornstalks. He lived in the steppes amidst the beasts and he was their friend.

A hunter from Uruk caught sight of Enkidu as he came down to a water hole with his animals, and at once he thought to himself: This man would be a match for Gilgamesh. The hunter went to his father for advice and the old man said: "I know how to entice this man away from the steppes and into the city. Take one of the priestesses from the temple with you to the water hole and she shall tempt the wild man, and teach him that he is not an animal but a man who is better living among people than with beasts."

When the priestess arrived at the water hole, she threw off her clothes before Enkidu and he burned with love for her and made her his wife. And now Enkidu became a stranger to the beasts in the steppes. The gazelles and other wild creatures of the desert fled from him. When Enkidu looked around, he saw that only his wife was left and she took him to Uruk.

On the way, she spoke to him thus: "Now you have grown wise and most like a god. In Uruk you will meet Gilgamesh and pit your strength against his."

"I am the strong one!" cried Enkidu.

"Let him see your face, this man of wrath, this man of misery, Gilgamesh," said the woman.

Then Gilgamesh was haunted by dreams, for he sensed the approach of Enkidu.

In Uruk, Enkidu learned the ways of mankind. He ate bread as men do and he drank the wine that men drink. He washed his body and put on clothes like other men. He became a shepherd and slew wolves and hunted lions, and he became a watchman, always on the alert.

Then a man from Uruk came to Enkidu and spoke to him. "A wedding feast will be held today, but Gilgamesh the king wants to take the bride for himself before the husband can lead her home to be his wife."

When Enkidu heard this, he grew pale with anger. He took up his stance in the market place to challenge Gilgamesh. He was shorter in stature than the king, but equal to him in strength, for he had fed on the spring herbs in the steppes and drunk the milk of wild beasts. As Gilgamesh drew near to carry off the bride for a night, Enkidu stepped forward barring the king's way. The two men flew at each other, and as they grappled, doorposts were shattered and walls were broken. They were locked together like bulls in combat, but when one had forced the other to his knees, all their anger melted and they stopped fighting.

Enkidu marveled at the strength of Gilgamesh, and he said, "Your head towers above those of all other men. It is right that Enlil has given you the kingship."

Then they embraced and sealed their friendship. Gilgamesh

*Gilgamesh overcomes a buffalo, cylinder seal, Mari, 3rd millenium* B.C. *(Damascus)*

led Enkidu to his mother, Ninsun, and said: "Here is another son for you, who is invincible. He has neither father nor mother and he was born in the steppes."

And to Enkidu he said: "Let us set off together now, to kill the monster Humbaba who lives in the forest of cedars. Let us wipe out evil from this land."

Enkidu was afraid and said: "When I used to wander through the cedar forest with the beasts, I saw Humbaba. His roar is like the deluge, his jaws are fire, his breath is death. No one can overcome him. Why do you seek certain death for your portion?"

Then said Gilgamesh: "Nothing shall prevent me from entering Humbaba's forest and felling the tallest cedar trees. You stay here, Enkidu. An axe will be my companion, that is all I need."

Once again Enkidu implored Gilgamesh: "Enlil himself has commanded Humbaba to guard the cedars. Whoever enters that forest will be paralysed with fear. His grave is dug."

"Which of us can climb to heaven?" retorted Gilgamesh. "That is only for the gods who reign there forever. Man is but a

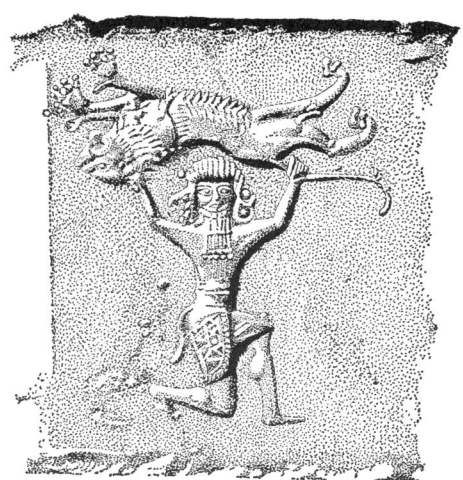

*Gilgamesh overcomes a lion, 3nd millenium* B.C. *(New York)*

breath of wind that blows. But is that a reason to shrink away from death and to shun danger? I shall challenge Humbaba to fight me, I shall fell the cedars that are his pride. And if I fall, my name will endure. I want to make a name for myself."

When Enkidu heard this, he no longer wanted to stay behind. And the armorers cast mighty axes for them and forged swords with hilts weighing thirty pounds apiece. Gilgamesh and Enkidu then set forth and stood before the gate with the seven bolts. The whole people assembled there and the elders of Uruk besought the king to change his mind.

"It is because you are so young that your heart has driven you to do this, Gilgamesh," they said. "You do not know what lies ahead of you." But when they saw that they could not make him alter his decision, they gave him some advice. "Let Enkidu go on ahead of you, he knows the way. He knows all the approaches and his eyes are bright."

"I hear your advice," said Gilgamesh, "but now we will go and see my mother."

Hand in hand with Enkidu, he went to the palace of his

mother, Ninsun, and he asked her to pray to the sun-god for help, so that they would succeed in felling the great cedars.

Ninsun donned the festive robe she wore for making sacrifice, and she sprinkled water on the earth and the dust. Then she climbed the steps to the roof of the palace, and raising her arms, she called on the god of the sun. "Why have you given my son a restless heart? Why have you roused in him the desire to kill Humbaba? For he does your will when he drives the evil which is hateful to you from the land. Therefore look down by day on the path that Gilgamesh treads, and let the watchers of darkness, the stars, gaze down on him at night; and in the evening, the moon-god."

After making sacrifice, Gilgamesh and Enkidu set out for the cedar forest. At the edge of the forest they came upon a watchman and they killed him in fight, although he was muffled in seven coats to protect himself from the blows of the sword.

They pushed on farther until they stood before the green mountain, following Humbaba's spoor. The height of the cedar trees left them speechless with awe but they went on until they stood in front of a thicket of thornbushes, as close-set as a wall. And Humbaba did not come forth.

Then said Enkidu: "As Humbaba will not show himself, we shall lure him to us with dreams, with strong dreams three times over."

They lay down to rest and Gilgamesh dreamed that a wild bull attacked him in the steppes and he sent the wild beast crashing to the ground. He awoke with a start and told Enkidu his dream. "It was Humbaba who came to you in the form of a wild bull," said Enkidu, "and you vanquished him." They traveled on for another day, as far as the next halt. In the middle of the night, Gilgamesh started up out of his sleep for the second time and turned to Enkidu. "Did you wake me, or was it my dream? Listen to what I dreamed. A mountain collapsed and fell upon me, and I was buried beneath it to the hips. Then there appeared a being made of light, who pulled me out from under the ruins and re-

*Head of a Woman, mid 4th millenium* B.C. (*Baghdad*)
*Following pages: Ram with the Tree of Life* (sometimes called *Ram caught in the Thicket*) *Ur, c. 2400* B.C. (*London*)
*Dignitaries offering a sacrifice, Fresco from Mari, c. 2000* B.C.

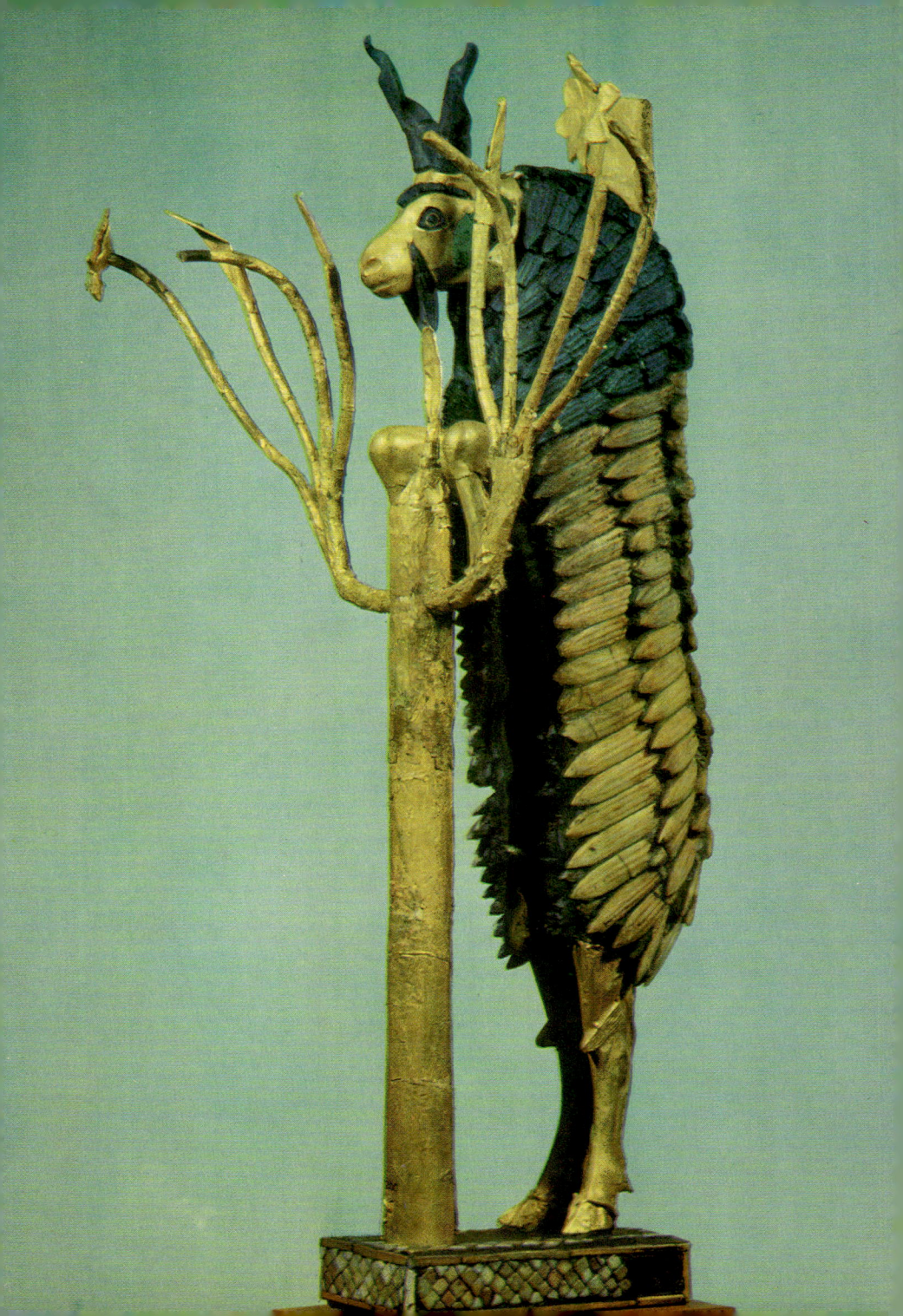

freshed me with cool water, and gave me firm ground beneath my feet once more." Joyfully Enkidu answered him, "The mountain was Humbaba. He must yield, we shall conquer him."

Again they journeyed on for yet another day, until they came to the highest cedars. They dug a well in the ground for water and they offered a sacrifice. The spreading branches of the cedar tree made a roof to protect them from the rain. Gilgamesh remained seated with his chin on his knees in order to stay awake, for he was frightened of dreaming once more. But in spite of this, sleep overtook him and for the third time he started up out of his dream and said to Enkidu: "Was it you who jolted me? Why am I stricken with horror, why do I tremble in every limb? Did some god pass this way? Listen to my dream. The heavens shrieked and darkness fell from the sky, which was riven asunder by the lightning. There was a rain of death and then suddenly the fire went out and all was turned to ashes." "Your dream is a good sign for you," said Enkidu. "It is Humbaba who will be turned to ashes. Now let us cut down the cedar tree."

This they did and as the cedar came crashing down, Humbaba ran out shouting: "Who is it who desecrates the cedar tree? Who fells the son of the mountains?" Gilgamesh and Enkidu blanched before Humbaba and his wrath, but then they heard the sun-god calling to them from the sky: "Step forth against him. Do not be afraid."

Eight great winds seized Humbaba: the great wind, the north wind, the whirlwind, the sandstorm, the hurricane, the frost wind, the thunderstorm, and the scorching simoom. They blew in his eyes and trapped him so that he could not move forward or backward. And when Gilgamesh attacked Humbaba, the wild watchman cried: "Stop, Gilgamesh! You shall be my master. I shall build houses for you from the cedars of the mountain." But Enkidu said: "We may not spare Humbaba." And the two men flung the net over the monster Humbaba and killed him. Then they washed their bodies and cleansed them from the dirt, and Gilgamesh put on the royal mantle. Radiant he stood there after

*Urnanshe, the singer, Mari, c. 2000* B.C. (*Damascus*)

the victory. This was how Inanna saw him, and she said to him: "Be my husband and your country will prosper."

But Gilgamesh remembered King Dumuzi, whom Inanna had despatched to the underworld, and he spurned the goddess. "To which husband are you faithful? You are an unfinished door that does not keep out the wind, you are the pitch that defiles the carrier, you are a jewel that entices the enemy into the land."

Offended by these words, Inanna entered the presence of her father, Anu. With tears in her eyes she asked him a favor: "Lend me the Bull of Heaven so that the city of Gilgamesh shall be destroyed." And she threatened that she would call up the demons of the underworld if Anu refused. So the god of the skies granted her her wish and the Bull of Heaven attacked Uruk. When he snorted, great fissures opened up in the ground and many people fell into these chasms and were crushed to death. But Gilgamesh and Enkidu overcame the Bull of Heaven, too. They struck it a blow between the horns and scruff of the neck and they tore out its heart. Then Enkidu cut off the bull's thighbone and flung it before Inanna's feet. For the goddess, this was an unspeakable outrage. She stepped before the gods and insisted that Enkidu should die for his sacrilege. He was stricken low by a grave sickness and in his delirium he cursed his fate before he died.

For seven days and seven nights did Gilgamesh mourn beside the corpse of his friend, and when Enkidu was buried, Gilgamesh called on Enki to help him. The wise god found a way to console even Gilgamesh. He had a window let into the underworld, and Enkidu was allowed to step through it into the light once more to embrace Gilgamesh. From the kingdom of the dead, Enkidu had nothing but ghastly things to report. Gilgamesh shuddered and when Enkidu stepped down into the pit again, Gilgamesh remained on earth, horror-stricken. Dressed in a lionskin, Gilgamesh fled blindly into the steppes. Panic seized him. He could see himself lying dead like his friend and he made up his mind to go to Utnapishtim, his ancestor, to ask him, the immortal one, for the secret of everlasting life.

Across mountain ranges and through the lands of darkness, Gilgamesh sought the way. For twelve hours long and another twelve hours he groped through the utter blackness and the north wind whipped his face. Then it grew light again. At the edge of the dry land stood a wine seller and she asked Gilgamesh: "Where are you running so fast? You will never find the eternal life you seek, for that is reserved for the gods. The lot of mankind is death. Therefore enjoy yourself while you may. You cannot reach the island of Paradise where Utnapishtim lives."

But Gilgamesh would not give in. At the water's edge he found the boatman whom Utnapishtim had taken with him into the ark; and with sixty strokes of the oars and yet another sixty, he ferried him over to the island that lies beyond death.

"Why have you come here?" asked Utnapishtim. "Why has the color drained from your cheeks?"

"Enkidu my friend is dead," answered Gilgamesh. "As he lay there before me, I shrank in horror at the putrefaction of the body. What must I do so as not to die? You must know the answer."

"Death is inexorable," Utnapishtim replied.

"But you live forever," Gilgamesh protested. "Am I not like you?"

Then Utnapishtim revealed to him the secret of the Flood. "To me alone have the gods given immortal life, because it was only through me that the human race survived."

"You must find a way for me, too, so that I shall never die," Gilgamesh insisted.

Utnapishtim then counseled him to fight off the desire to sleep for six days and seven nights, but that was too much for Gilgamesh. Sleep wrapped itself about him like a thick mist, so that Utnapishtim's wife had pity on him. She woke him up and baked him seven loaves for the journey home. Then Gilgamesh lamented: "Death is already clutching at my heart. It lurks in my sleeping chamber. Wherever I set my foot, everywhere, death lies in wait for me."

At this, Utnapishtim relented and revealed to him a secret that

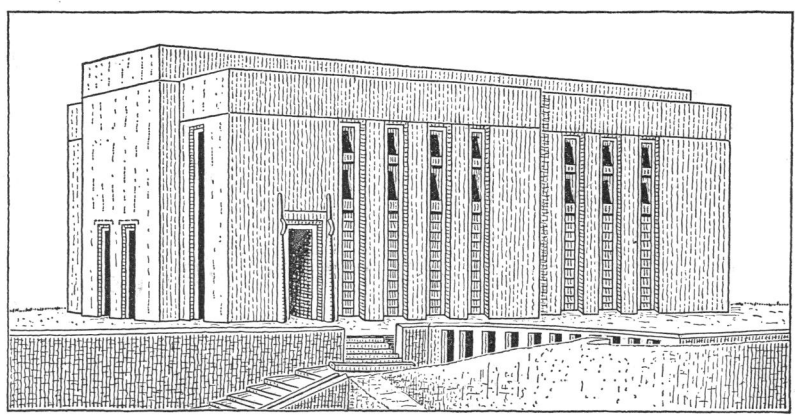

*Temple in Uruk (Reconstruction after E. Heinrich)*

he alone knew. "At the bottom of the sea there grows an herb whose name is 'The-old-grow-young-again,' " he said. "You may go and fetch it."

Gilgamesh bound heavy stones to his feet and dived down to the sea bed. He found the herb and rose to the surface with it. The waves cast him ashore, and full of joy he set off on the journey home to Uruk, holding the plant of eternal youth in his hand. The ferryman went with him.

After thirty hours and yet another thirty, Gilgamesh wished to refresh himself and so he bathed in a well of water. A serpent nearby smelled the sweet odor of the herb that lay at the rim of the well. It glided up to the plant and devoured it. Then it sloughed its skin and vanished. When Gilgamesh realized what had happened, bitter tears flowed down his cheeks. "For whom have I toiled so?" he cried aloud. "For whom have I shed my heart's blood? It was not for myself but for the snake that I fetched the herb of eternal youth. I have nothing left, nothing for myself after diving to the bottom of the sea!"

"Let us go to Uruk," said the ferryman. "You will find comfort there."

And so they came to the city, and when Gilgamesh saw the gleaming wall which circled Uruk that had been built according to his will, he looked at it with pride. "Climb to the top of the wall," he said to the ferryman. "Test the brickwork! Within its confines are gardens of palm trees, the valley, and the temple precincts. The Seven Wise Men laid the foundation for my wall."

And at the sight of the wall, joy returned to the heart of Gilgamesh. It was through this, his handiwork, that he did indeed conquer time and death.

# The Secret of Ur

Gilgamesh was a rebel. He thought it unfair that men had to face a worse fate than the gods who relied on men for their sustenance. It was the gods who had made the rivers in such a way that they threatened the Land of Ur year by year; it was only through the system of canals built by men that the land became habitable. It was the gods who had created men so that they attacked one another in war. It was only by man-built walls that the cities became safe places to live in.

"We improve your work, but instead of sharing your immortality with us, you dole out Death as our portion," Gilgamesh reproached the gods. "You are unjust."

The kings of Ur who followed the first dynasty of Uruk as rulers of the Land of Sumer and their people sought a different way of escaping from the transient nature of life. Evidence for this was found by the men who excavated Ur. The hill in which this ancient city was discovered is called by the Arabs "Tell el Muqayyar," which means the "Mound of Pitch." The Arabs gave it this name because they came upon so much bitumen there in the course of robbing the graves. This bitumen, or pitch, had been used as mortar for the buildings of the lost city. The *tell* lies about two hundred miles inland, but Ur, the venerable city hidden beneath the mound, was once close to the sea, which has gradually receded through the ages. Muqayyar was identified as the location of Ur as long ago as 1853, but it is only since 1922 that its secrets have been wrested from their burial place. A

British team of archaeologists under the leadership of Sir Leonard Woolley was responsible for the dig there, an excavation that went on for many years.

Looking east from the mound, the eye is caught by a fringe of palm treetops marking the course of the Euphrates. To the south looms the *tell* that holds the ruins of Eridu. In this direction, and to the west and north also, there is nothing but a waste of sand. Nothing grows here, not even scrub.

Woolley began by digging trenches close to the "Sacred Area" of Ur. Once, a wall had been built as a retaining terrace for the temple, and alongside this wall had sprawled a huge graveyard, one that had come into use as long ago as 3000 B.C. In the course of centuries it had become derelict, but about one thousand years later, it was used for burials for the second time, and contemporary grave robbers took the opportunity to loot the much older tombs. Everything was confused, and often the lower strata were left uppermost, making the work of the archaeologists much more difficult. Both the original cemetery and the more recent one must each have contained the best part of a thousand graves for the common people. Among the grave goods that came to light were simple vessels and weapons, pieces of jewelry and seals.

Toward the end of the first season's dig, Woolley came upon a walled tomb that had been dug at a deeper level. It was clear from the start that there was promise here of some exceptionally rewarding finds, but Woolley made an astonishing decision. He had the "gold trench," as it was known, carefully filled in again with earth and abandoned for the time being; he then moved on to excavate elsewhere. He was ready to forego the likelihood of a speedy and sensational discovery because his Arab workmen were not yet experienced enough to do the job satisfactorily. They had first to learn, for instance, to recognize where decayed sticks or poles once stood by noticing a row of holes in the ground; or to trace the edge of reed matting by no more than a wavy line of white powder. They had to be taught how to wield a pick without disturbing the arrangement of the finds; and how to improvise an awning of cloaks with a flick of the wrist when a sudden shower of rain threatened to reduce everything in a trench to slime.

Woolley's first move was to start conscientiously sorting out the two thousand graves, a task, he says, that "became wearisome at times." But it was only thus that the necessary depth of experience could be gained. A sharper contrast to the practice of Botta, Layard, and Rassam cannot be imagined. They, on the one hand, were impatience itself, determined to dig out as many valuable objects as they could in the shortest possible time. Woolley, on the other hand, resigned himself to years of meticulous and laborious spadework, concerned only with how to produce the most accurate picture obtainable of a world that had vanished thousands of years ago.

It was only in the winter of 1927, after five years of "apprenticeship," that the team went back to the spot they had noted as a special grave. Woolley's patience was richly rewarded. Hardly was the tomb opened when they found a copper spear tip sticking straight up in the ground. Its shaft had decayed, leaving a long slender hollow in the earth below the tip. More spears were found blade down, and between them lay vases of alabaster and clay. In the center of the grave chamber stood a coffin with various objects around it: a shield, two gold-mounted daggers, chisels and other tools, copper jugs, silver bowls, and a set of arrows.

The dead man lay on his right side. He wore a broad silver belt from which hung a gold dagger and a whetstone of lapis lazuli. The coffin was covered with a mass of beads of gold and semiprecious stones. Golden bowls had been placed between the corpse's hands, near his left elbow, and behind his head; by the right shoulder there was a double axehead of electrum. Behind him were heaped many articles: bracelets, earrings and spirals of gold, as well as various amulets. By far the finest piece, however, was a helmet of beaten gold in the form of a wig with

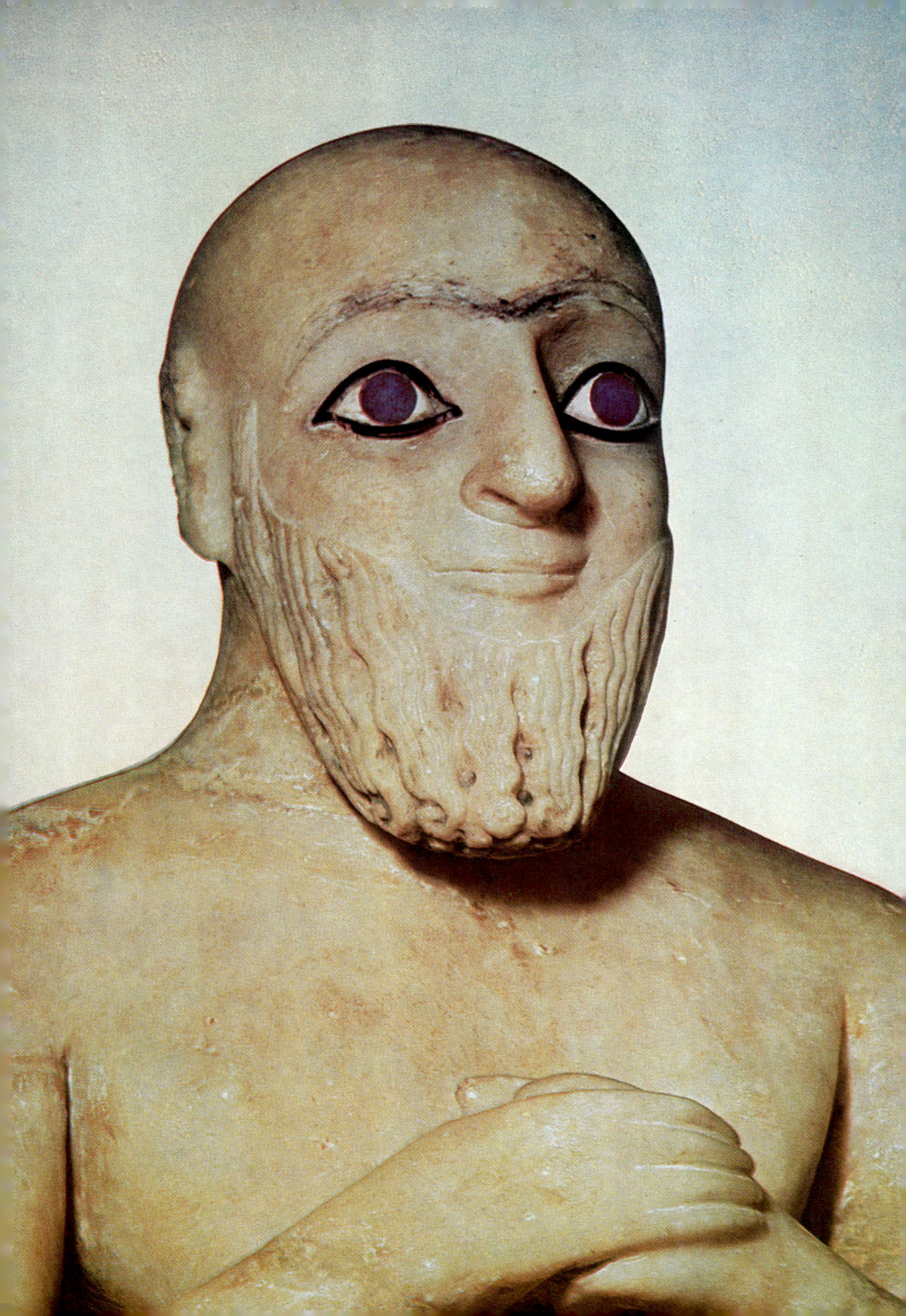

a most elaborate hair style. There was a knot of hair tied at the back, a twisted plait and a headband, and guards for ears and cheeks. It was a specimen of the goldsmith's art of the highest order.

Two gold dishes and a lamp, however, were even more important for the archaeologist, for on them was inscribed the name of the man who had found his "eternal dwelling" in this tomb. He was Meskalamdug, the Hero of the Good Land. Presumably he was a prince and not a king, for there was no

*Gold dagger with lapis-lazuli hilt and filigree sheath, Ur, 3000 B.C. (Baghdad)*

*Opposite page: Gaming Board, Ur, c. 2500 B.C. (Philadelphia)*

sign of a title of royalty either there or on the cylinder seal with his name that was found later in a queen's grave.

Soon after the opening of Meskalamdug's tomb, the expedition came upon the royal tombs themselves. On the floor of one shaft lay many copper weapons, but among them was an outstandingly beautiful golden dagger. The lapis-lazuli hilt was chased with gold and decorated with gold studs, and its golden sheath had a rich filigree pattern through which the blade could be seen. Nearby was a slim pointed container with tweezers and other toilet instruments, all made of gold. Not far away, a number of limestone slabs were exposed. At first, Woolley thought that this was some kind of paving, but later it became clear that these slabs had once formed the roof of a royal vault. Grave robbers had ransacked the tomb leaving only a few vessels behind.

In a nearby section the expedition opened a ruined grave in which lay the skeletons of five men with copper daggers at their waists and small clay cups beside them. The floor of the grave revealed traces of matting. By following these powdery marks the team came to a shaft where lay the remains of ten women carefully arranged in two rows. All had headdresses of gold, lapis lazuli, and carnelian as well as bead necklaces. At the end of the row were the remains of a wonderful harp or lyre, decorated with gold, and a sounding box edged with a mosaic of red and blue stones, and with a bull's head wrought in gold with eyes and beard of lapis. After this, the discoveries came thick and fast. A little way inside the shaft entrance they found the queen's carriage, a vehicle like a sledge, with decorations in red, white, and blue mosaic and golden lions' heads. In front of the sledge were the bones of the two asses that had drawn it. The reins had passed through a double ring of silver, on which stood a little mascot, a small golden donkey. Beside the sledge lay a collection of tools and weapons, bowls of soapstone, vessels of copper, silver, volcanic glass, alabaster and marble, and gold goblets as well. There was also a golden saw, an object of the highest significance. When remnants of a decayed wooden chest were removed, a brick vault was discovered below. The roof had been broken through and the hole was big enough for a man to climb down into the chamber.

The team then dug out an approach to this chamber and found a ramp leading to it, with six soldiers at its foot. They wore copper helmets and spears and were lying in two orderly rows. There were also two large wagons each drawn by three oxen. Against the wall of the chamber lay nine women wearing the gala headdress of lapis and carnelian beads from which hung golden pendants.

The chamber with a hole in the roof contained the skeletons of no less than sixty-three men and women. All the dead were laden with adornments. There were also the remains of a second harp with gold mountings and a bull's head, and four shell plaques with pictures on them. These engravings show scenes in which animals play human parts, performing as clowns or musicians. It was obvious that courtiers had been buried in the grave beside the king, but there was no trace of his body, although a cylinder seal revealed his name: Abargi.

Near the royal vault a burial chamber had been built for the queen. Her name was discovered on a lapis-lazuli seal; she was called Shubad. The arched roof of her grave chamber had caved in and made a protective covering for the body of the dead consort and the lavish furnishings of her grave. Here were massed a profusion of beads made of gold and semiprecious stones, gold pins, gazelles of gold and a headdress of golden flowers whose petals were inlaid with white and gold. A golden comb was stuck in her hair, and close by lay a second headdress of an unusual sort. Onto a diadem made apparently of a strip of soft white leather had been sewn thousands of minute lapis-lazuli beads, and against this background of solid blue was set a row of exquisitely fashioned gold animals—stags, gazelles, bulls, and goats —with clusters of pomegranates between them, three fruits hanging together shielded by their leaves, and branches of some other tree with golden stems and fruit of gold and carnelian,

*Gold helmet of Meskalamdug, Ur, 3rd millenium* B.C. *(Baghdad)*

while gold rosettes were sewn on at intervals. At the head and the foot of the bier on which the queen had been laid to rest crouched two women attendants. All round the chamber were strewn bowls of gold, silver, copper, and stone. There were lamps and a number of little cockle shells with green, white, and red paint in them which had, presumably, been used for makeup. No grave robber had desecrated the contents of this tomb.

In the king's vault there were also precious treasures, among them two small boats, one of silver and the other of copper. The silver one was extremely well-preserved. It was about two feet long, with a high prow and stern. There were five seats, an arched support for an awning, and oars with blades shaped like leaves.

In Woolley's opinion, the boats and a number of other valuable objects, such as a gaming board, must have been overlooked by the grave robbers. He was convinced that these robbers had broken in through the hole in the roof, yet neither the queen nor the sixty-three men and women of the royal train had been robbed. Fairy-tale riches lay there untouched.

Two questions present themselves. Why was it that only the body of the king appeared to be missing from the grave that housed so many corpses? And why were there so many people buried in the grave prepared for a king and queen? The circumstances of the find left only one possible explanation: These men and women had followed King Abargi and Queen Shubad voluntarily to their deaths.

In all there were sixteen graves discovered in Ur where kings were buried with a large retinue. In none of these was there any sign of panic or the use of violence. Only the pressure of the earth had disturbed the elaborate headdresses of the women, not one skull showed evidence of the slightest injury. The harp players' fingers still touched the strings. These men and women had died as if they were falling into a deep sleep. They had worn bright red robes and were heavily adorned with fine jewelry. They had gone down into the death-pit as if they were going to a great feast. They had felt themselves secure from the horror of dying and had had no hesitation in drinking the narcotic or poison the priests had prepared and poured out for them from copper kettles.

One princess must have been only about seven years old. A separate grave had been prepared for her and the jewelry she wore was as fine as that of Queen Shubad, only the pieces were all in miniature and much more delicate. Tiny gold leaves and rings decorated her hair, her childish hand held a golden cup only two inches high. All the grave gifts were faithful imitations copied from those of the queen. This princess belonged to one of the select band who had to be equipped for "the life beyond" with everything they were used to in this life.

*Rein-rings
with wild ass, Ur,
3rd millenium* B.C.
*(London)*

For the courtiers of these early kings of Ur, the departure from this earth was a transition from one sphere to another, where everything endured and whose glory was imperishable. For the king was returning to the realm of the gods whence he had come. According to Sumerian belief, the kingship "was sent down from on high." The king did not die, he was transformed into a divine personage. Whoever accompanied him when he took this step would share in the immortality which the king was entering. Death was not the end but a door to eternal life. A Sumerian felt more secure from mortality in the immediate vicinity of his king than anywhere else.

But where had the king gone, since he was no longer in his vault? The most significant of the grave gifts, the golden saw, reveals the secret. It was the sun-god who was usually symbolized by the saw. Morning after morning he sawed his way out of the prison of the night to climb the mountains in the east. There he shone in radiance, celebrating his daily marriage to the earth. The dead king, too, sawed his way out of the grave when the time came. For him, too, there was a wedding after death. And the living assisted him in his return to the kingdom of light. After a certain space of time, perhaps on the day on which the queen was united with her husband in death, a window was broken in the roof of his burial vault and his body was brought out.

The sun-god was not the only model for the kings of Ur. The shepherd-king Dumuzi also rose perpetually from the underworld to solemnize a new marriage to Inanna so that life should flourish on earth.

As long as they lived, this holy wedding was the great annual event for all the kings of Sumer. At the Feast of the New Year, the entire population celebrated the victory of life over death.

*The god Shamash, cylinder seal, 3rd millenium* B.C. *(London)*

# Temple Towers

Seventy years before Sir Leonard Woolley arrived on the spot, another Englishman, J. E. Taylor, had done some digging at Ur. At Rawlinson's suggestion, he drove a tunnel into the northern section of the Hill of Muqayyar and he came upon a vast building made of mud bricks and solid right through. Taylor established that it had had two stories, but his Arab workmen said they were certain that "in days of yore" there had been a third tier. When Taylor dug deeper, he found a stratum of bricks with rounded tops like the ones used for building the wall of Uruk. Digging deeper still, he came upon the prismatic *Riemchen* bricks, the oldest shape we know. This was proof that there had been building and rebuilding on that same site for many hundreds of years. What Taylor had found were the remains of a stepped, or terraced, temple tower, a *ziggurat,* as it is called. During the 1920s Woolley needed a whole army of laborers working for several years to free it from the shroud of rubble and sand that had buried it for so long.

So far, thirty-three of these stepped towers have been discovered in the Land of the Two Rivers, distributed among twenty-seven cities. Ancient records mention other ziggurats in cities that have not yet been excavated. One odd fact is that in many cities that have been thoroughly explored, such as Nineveh, there is no sign of such towers.

The first person to excavate a stepped tower was Sir Henry Layard, at Nimrud, although he did not go deep enough to obtain a clear picture of the ziggurat of old Calah. Fifty years later, Dr. Robert Koldewey dug out the Tower of Babel. He found only a few ruins, for Alexander the Great had ordered the demolition of everything that remained of the mighty edifice in his day, and the ground water at the base proved to be too high to allow Koldewey to penetrate into deeper strata. But he was able to reconstruct a plan of the stepped tower with a fair degree of certainty, and he established that a temple had once stood on the topmost terrace.

Why were stepped towers like these built in the Land of the Two Rivers? That is the question the archaeologists asked, amazed at the dimensions of these structures. Some of them suggested that these were sanctuaries or shrines built on one or more foundations in order to protect them from flooding, and the idea is not so farfetched. Even today, after a sudden cloudburst, the *tells* which house the temples stand out like islands above the surface of the floodwaters. In Sumerian times, however, they had a more efficient protection against flooding, not only for temples but even for ordinary dwelling houses; that is, the system of canals and dikes, which even safeguarded the cultivated land in the low-lying plains.

These Sumerian and Babylonian temples have two particularly striking features. They had many gateways and long flights of steps leading to the top. Nowadays the highest story of almost all the stepped towers have fallen into decay, and the top portion of the stairway has completely disappeared. However, in one of the shrines in Uruk the top step has been preserved. This step is well over three feet high.

No human being could mount such a high step in one stride, that is obvious, so it cannot have been intended for a man at all, but for a god. It was for the divinity to set his foot on when he descended from heaven. Since innumerable hymns to Sumerian gods have been deciphered, there is no doubt about the purpose of the towers. These towers, with their grand stairways, were built to make it easier for the gods to come down to earth. Most

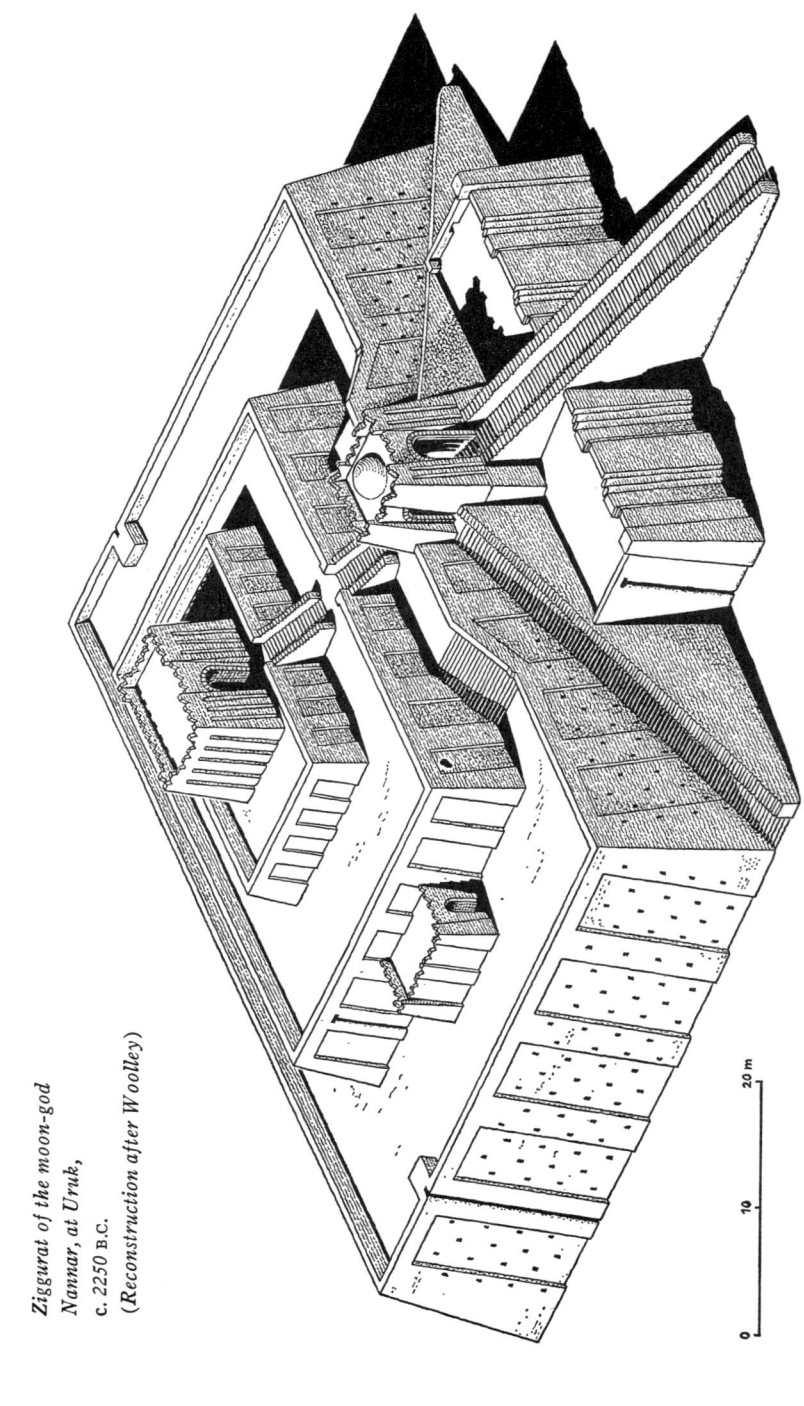

Ziggurat of the moon-god
Nannar, at Uruk,
c. 2250 B.C.
(Reconstruction after Woolley)

of all, they were reception ramps for the goddess Inanna. The temple on top of the highest terrace was the bridal chamber where the king awaited the arrival of the goddess. Here was the meeting place of those exalted beings, to renew the ancient alliance. This is confirmed by the name that has been handed down for these towers. The ziggurat of Larsa is called The House of the Bond between Heaven and Earth. The name of the city with the greatest tower of all, Babylon, means "the Gateway of the Gods."

Gazing up to the temple at the top of the ziggurat, mankind looked out over the earth. There, year after year, was celebrated the fabled wedding between the shepherd-king Dumuzi and the goddess Inanna, the queen of heaven—to everyone's delight. It was Dumuzi who replenished the meadows. He was the protector of flocks and herds; he provided for their fodder and defended them against lions and the eagle Imdugud, the bird of death. Dumuzi is the manly "hero of the good land"; he wards off evil and destruction.

On many stone plaques with a hole bored through the center, Dumuzi and Inanna are shown together. The king and goddess sit facing one another, sharing one cup or drinking from a two-spouted jug. Around them are servants, dancers, and musicians, and laden carts and boats bring offerings to them. There are competitions and games. Clowns divert the spectators and wrestlers, balancing jars on their heads, go into a clinch. The general rejoicing increases, the excitement mounts. Servants are made equal with the mighty. And while the true king goes into retreat, communing with himself and remaining invisible to his people, the festival king, a commoner, rules over them and his commands have all the authority of the king's.

There are seal impressions and engravings showing two animals sitting opposite each other like the divine bride and groom, drinking from the double-spouted jug. Others perform as tumblers or musicians. Obviously the Sumerians did not consider it offensive to have animals acting the part of gods. The

*Decoration on front of lyre, Ur, c. 3000 B.C. (Philadelphia)*

lion and the bull, the goat and the eagle alike were all citizens in the realm of the gods, everything was sanctified by the divine breath of the wise god Enki. To him the Sumerians sacrificed in their homes, placing their offerings down the drains! They did not consider this unseemly, for they were not at all squeamish. They were a robust people who thought in practical terms. The domestic sewers seemed to them a sensible approach to the "god of the watery deeps," and any means were justified if they ensured that Enki did not starve.

In the eyes of the Sumerians the sacred nature of the yearly wedding between Dumuzi and Inanna was not in any way diminished by the fact that it was consummated by the king and queen instead. To them, the king was Dumuzi himself, risen from the dead. They put their trust in him exactly as they did in the gods. They felt secure in the protection of the good shepherd who ever and again broke out of the region of the dead, and in the grace and favor of the queen of heaven who came down to earth every year to meet him.

The temple, which was open on all sides and could be reached by several flights of steps, offered more security than the wall with the thousand watchtowers built by Gilgamesh, protesting against mortality but deaf to the laments of his people. Gilgamesh seems like a stranger among the kings of Sumer. Missing from his character was that submission to the decree of the gods that was considered the supreme virtue of the Land of Ur.

The Sumerians were a pious people. They enjoyed visiting their temples. Within, the temples were shrines of great magnificence. Apart from the colored clay-peg (or wall-cone) mosaics, they were adorned with friezes of gold and colored stones, with copper panels, marble rosettes, and inlays. The citizens presented as votive offerings figures of stone and metal: lions, gazelles, eagles, hedgehogs, and scorpions. They commissioned images of themselves as "worshipers" so that they could be present in the sanctuary even when they were needed in the fields or at the canals or in the workshops. The "worshipers" (images) represented them before the altar.

*Copper figures,
two wrestlers balancing jars
on their heads,
c. 3200 B.C. (Baghdad)*

These figures—in all sizes—have been found in almost every excavation site. In 1934, an American team in Tell Asmar discovered twelve undamaged alabaster statuettes beneath the floor of a very early shrine. They had obviously been buried to make room for new figures, but care was taken that at least they remained within the sacred precincts, like the "king in the jug" found by the German expedition at the shrine of Inanna in Uruk.

In the temple of Inanna in Nippur, the Americans came upon four different sets of "worshipers" in the 1960–61 season. In all, fifty such figures were found. They are so strikingly alike that they might all be members of the same family. They all wear the same wraparound skirts edged with a border of sheepskin tufts. The upper part of the body is almost always bared, although occasionally one of them has a stole thrown over one shoulder. Often their hair is plastered with bitumen which makes it seem black and glossy. The eyes look like gaping holes, even when the shell disks that were commonly inset have remained in place.

These "worshipers" make us keep our distance—they are lost in prayer. Everything trivial has been discarded, there is no partition between them and eternity, no fear of death. They share in the glory that unites the resurrected Dumuzi and Inanna. It was because of this union that the Land of Sumer flourished. There were wars, true, but the people strove with all their might to make the land between the rivers into a garden of paradise. Unlike the nations to the east, west, and north, the Sumerians wanted nothing but to live in peace and go about their work.

# Of Farmers, Builders, and Others

The largest of the sixteen royal graves that Sir Leonard Woolley found in Ur had already been broken into by grave robbers and thoroughly ransacked. The team removed a layer of earth many feet thick without coming across any important finds, until only one corner remained to be excavated.

To their surprise, a loose piece of shell was seen, and a little later they saw the corner of a mosaic pattern of lapis lazuli, red limestone, and pearl. With the greatest caution the soil was removed crumb by crumb and one after the other the fragments gleamed forth. The stones were all loose in the ground, for the wooden frame that had once held them together had long since disappeared without a trace. Falls of earth and stone had made the mosaic rise here and sag there, but the pieces which made up the whole had preserved their positions in relation to each other. It was a problem to know how to remove all the dirt without disturbing anything. To do so needed the eyes of a hawk and the most delicate touch. Only one square inch at a time could be tackled. As each minute portion was exposed, hot wax was poured over it to bind the fragments together, but inevitably the wax mingled with the dirt and, temporarily at least, the picture disappeared beneath a coating of mud.

But when at last the whole tablet had been preserved in this way and could be lifted out, the expedition knew that they had made an exceptionally valuable find. As the panel had been lying by a man's shoulder and had once had a wooden pole attached

88 *Detail from the Standard of Ur—"Peace"—c. 2500* B.C. *(London)*
*Following pages: Detail from the Standard of Ur—"War"—c. 2500* B.C *(London)*
*Bull's Head, Lyre decoration, Ur. c. 2500* B.C. *(Baghdad)*

to it, Woolley was reminded of a banner carried in procession on festive occasions, and so he called the find the Standard of Ur.

There were mosaic illustrations on both sides of the panel. Against a gleaming background of blue lapis are several rows of figures. In order to keep the pieces in their right order the panel was laid on a sheet of glass as it was, the wax was then warmed and the particles of dirt were fished out one by one. At the same time the pieces were coaxed together by pressure from the sides. The process was repeated on the reverse side and now the whole picture emerged clearly.

On one side there are soldiers wearing helmets and stiff cloaks, marching to war with spears and battle axes. At the bottom is a row of four war chariots going into battle. The team in the rear is trotting along at a sedate pace, but the ones drawing the other chariots are traveling at ever increasing speeds, and one of the leading chariots has its wheels rolling over the bodies of fallen enemy soldiers. Each team is whipped on by its charioteers, inciting the beasts to tear into the ranks of the foe. The men fling light spears that stand ready to hand in quivers. The top register shows prisoners being led before the king; some of them are naked, others wear kilts with a zigzag hemline. The king has stepped down from his chariot, but even standing on the ground, he towers above the others.

*Engraved shell plaques, Telloh, 3rd millenium* B.C. *(London)*

*Opposite page: Eridu, remains of Ziggurat of Urnammu*

The reverse side of the panel depicts the victory celebration. The vanquished bring tribute, wild asses, bales of goods, meat and fish. The king sits on his throne wearing his sheepskin shirt. There is drinking, music, and rejoicing. Everyone is happy because the land is safe and danger has been averted.

What a contrast these scenes are to the relief carvings taken from the palaces of the kings of Assyria, with their scenes of the utmost cruelty and their glorification of war. The Standard of Ur extols a life of peace. In the Sumerian world it was not the soldiers who enjoyed the highest prestige and it is rare for the king to be shown as a leader of his troops. Much more often, he is pictured as a lawgiver or architect, even as a laborer at the building of a temple; or as a cultivator of crops or as a stockbreeder.

In 1950, an American expedition at Nippur dug out a tablet that was only three inches wide and four and a half inches long. It was more than thirty-five hundred years old, and on it was an important portion of a "farmer's almanac." Eight fragments of this agricultural "manual" had come to light beforehand, and now the complete text could be put together. Three Sumerologists—Kramer, Landsberger, and Jacobsen—made a joint translation of it and here is the gist of its contents:

In days of yore, a farmer gave his son these instructions: "Before you till your fields, open the sluices of the irrigation ditches but take care not to inundate the fields too much. When you water the land, make sure that the surface remains even; it should be as flat as a board.

"Do not allow the wandering oxen to churn up the soil; chase away any intruders immediately. Then prepare the fields for sowing. Clear the weeds with a pick and tear out the stubble by hand. If the ground scorches in the sun, divide it into four parts and then water them one at a time so that you are not held up in your work. Wield your tools with such energy that they sing. Even the children of your servants should help with such work as repairing baskets, or mending the bar of the yoke or a broken whip. Before you begin to plough, break up the earth twice with the mattock and once with the hoe. If need be, use a hammer in order to demolish the toughest clods. Roll the field flat and fence it round. And keep an eye on your laborers.

"When you are ploughing, take care that your ploughshare cuts deep enough into the ground. The grains should fall two fingers deep in the earth from the seeder you have fastened to the plough. Set the new furrows diagonally to last year's furrows and be sure that no clods of earth fall into the furrows and make it difficult for the seed to germinate.

"On the day that the field turns green, say a prayer to the goddess of field mice and other vermin so that they will spare your crops. Scare away those winged thieves, the birds. When the corn is as high as a mat, give it water. Then open the irrigation sluices twice more and once again, four times in all. When the corn stands at its full strength, cut it. Let the threshing sledge pass over the ears until they are empty. The grain must then be winnowed until it is free from all dirt and impurity. Finally, remember that although these counsels issue from my mouth, they have been handed down by the god of meadows, who is the son of Enlil."

Market gardening was also practiced with great skill. To shield the growing plants from the burning glare of the sun and from the hot winds that blew from the desert, *sarbatu* trees were planted. Their leaves were as big as one's hand and provided the shade that was needed.

When the date palms blossomed, young boys would climb to the tops and stroke them with fans. This assisted pollination and ensured an abundant crop of dates. The farmers and gardeners to whom the soil of Sumer was entrusted utilized every foot of earth.

These people had plenty of common sense and a decided sense of humor, as we can tell from their numerous proverbs. Here are some of their sayings that have been handed down: "A thousand head of cattle give a heap of dung"; "No one gives away a cow for nothing"; "When the ox is groomed, the dog barks at it"; "Only the donkey eats its own bedding straw."

The earth was so fertile that it was too valuable to be left as pasture. Cows, asses, and sheep were fed with barley and waste products from the breweries. Oxen and asses worked the pumps to extract the water needed from the ground.

The common people lived modestly in the Land of Sumer as we know from their records and other finds. Their meals consisted mainly of barley, gruel, dates, honey and cheese, sesame oil and eggs, and they ate geese, ducks, hens—and locusts. They also cooked beef, pork, mutton, and goat flesh, but meat was something of a luxury. As there was little wood available, dung was used as fuel.

Fishing was an important industry in the Land of the Two Rivers and even pelicans were trained to catch fish. Fish were so plentiful that such delicacies as carp could be exported. It was more profitable to go fishing than hunting, but all the same, they chased hare and boar, the wild goat and wild sheep, antelope, gazelle and deer, ibex and the wild bull. There was fowling too, in all regions, but lion hunting was the king's prerogative.

Apart from hunters and fishermen, farmers and market gardeners, the Sumerians naturally had many other trades as well. There were bakers and butchers, brewers and cooks, basket makers and potters, masons and sculptors, carpenters and cartwrights, tailors and barbers, priests and doctors, teachers and scribes, bailiffs, overseers, shipbuilders and architects.

It was in building, however, that the Sumerians reached some of their highest achievements. Instead of stone they used mud bricks, with asphalt as mortar. As there were great buildings erected in all the towns, the demand for bricks was enormous. Sun-dried bricks made up the inner core of walls, and for cladding kiln-baked clay slabs were used. These Sumerian brickmakers certainly knew their business. Professor Edward Chiera tells of an English architect who visited Ur during a dig and wanted to take home with him a baked slab containing an inscription in high relief. This brick measured twelve inches square by three inches thick, and as the visitor only wanted the inscription, he thought he would hack away the plain part at the back with an axe. After half an hour's strenuous effort, the brick was still intact and the architect had to give up.

*Sumerian ploughing scene (after S. N. Kramer)*

Wherever they dug, the archaeologists found the remains of drainpipes, for the country was criss-crossed with a network of irrigation canals. The Sumerians knew how to provide drainage as well, and by means of a carefully devised system of clay pipes, they made sure that rain soaking into walls and foundations would be piped away before it could damage the fabric of the building.

The biggest feats of construction were carried out by slave labor. Slaves were either kidnapped from neighboring lands, or prisoners of war were forced into servitude after defeat in battle. Slaves had to do as they were told without protest. Unlike free men, they were not allowed to have two names. Their father's name was taken from them, for they were no longer members of a family. If someone injured a slave, the culprit had to pay compensation to the slave's owner and not to the victim. The usual price for a slave was the same as that for a cow, but at times it cost less to buy a slave than an ass. If a slave escaped and was recaptured, he was shackled hand and foot from then on. It was hard labor for them all.

But the farmers, the free craftsmen, and government officials —everyone in Sumer up to and including the king—worked hard to perform their untiring duty to the gods, the true rulers of the land. The building of walls from countless millions of bricks, the digging and dredging of canals as broad as rivers, the cultivation of a land that was threatened with flooding year by year, could only succeed "by agreement with Heaven," and by the devoted application of everyone's powers. Men of all callings vied with one another so that the storehouses were kept filled. Meticulous bookkeeping, balancing income and expenditure, was of great importance, and many of the priests held posts as scribes. The schools, where the study of the art of writing was considered the most important subject, were situated close beside the temple. Teaching and learning alike were performed under the eyes of the god.

# Of Schools and Scribes

In the autumn of 1949, the Americans resumed their excavations in Nippur. On the site where the temple to Enlil had stood, they found the remains of five temples, one built on top of the other, all built to the same ground plan. Here, on the most sacred spot in the whole of Sumer, it was obvious that nothing might be altered but only restored. In the shrine of the supreme god, Enlil, stood the throne from which the kingship derived its authority.

From the nearby Hill of Tablets many important texts had already been extracted. Now another seven hundred specimens were found. This encouraged the excavators, in the winter 1951–52, to dig down to virgin soil at two places. In doing so, they were able to identify twenty different building periods. On January 21, another cache with clay tablets was brought to light, and hundreds of inscribed tablets of small size were unearthed, among them two hundred containing poems and epics.

Hilprecht, who had led the excavations in Nippur before 1900 and had made some important finds of tablets himself, was convinced that they had come upon a temple library. This proved incorrect, but the inscriptions had come from a number of smallish collections that had stood side by side in a restricted space, that is they came from private libraries that the priests had kept in their own living quarters. These priests' libraries were also schools of writing, for in addition to many beautifully written texts, great numbers of childish school exercises were identifiable.

The schools were called "tablet houses" in ancient Mesopotamia. In Mari, a magnificent royal residence on the middle Euphrates, French archaeologists excavated two more tablet houses. The school benches were still standing, bare rows of forms made of mud bricks that quickly crumbled once they were exposed to the wind and the rain. Three thousand years before, the "sons of the tablet house," the pupils, had sat upon them and the "father of the tablet house," the headmaster, had tried to instruct them in the difficult art of writing cuneiform script.

That there must have been schools as early as 4000 B.C. can be deduced from the vocabularies found at Uruk. In the Flood city of Shuruppak, numbers of school exercises were dug up dating from the middle of the third millennium. We have examples of the written work done by pupils throughout the centuries that followed; they come from almost every excavation site. They range from beginners' scribblings to the finished copies executed by the most proficient pupils, so good that they can hardly be distinguished from the originals.

Education was obviously expensive. Only prosperous people could afford to send their sons to the tablet house, for the father's profession was always stated at the end of the text after the writer's own name. Thus we read that these scribes were the sons of mayors, ambassadors, temple dignitaries, officers, principals of libraries and of tablet houses. There is not a single tablet written by a woman, so there were clearly no girls in Sumerian schools.

The pupils were called "sons" by their teachers. To assist the school father there were "big brothers," supervisors or monitors for the various school subjects, which seem to have included drawing, arithmetic, and Sumerian. There was also the "big brother with the stick."

There were a great number of signs to be mastered, as many as two thousand in the earliest days, and the path to perfection, that is, to completing immaculate copies of fables, parables, hymns, and epics, was beset with thorns. Sumerian schoolboys

*Paintings on saucers, Samarra (restored), 5th millenium* B.C.

had to occupy those hard school benches for many a long year.

Among the compositions found is one that describes a typical school day. These sentences had to be written for practice by every pupil at one time or another, probably not just once but over and over again until the monitor was satisfied and praised the result. It was very easy to correct mistakes on these clay tablets. One had only to smooth them over with the stylus, or to scrape off the surface. True, the tablet grew thinner with each scraping, but when it got too thin, the pupil simply made himself a new one, which was quite easy. To keep the tablet soft enough to take an impression, all one had to do was to moisten it.

Here is one account of a day at school, somewhat compressed:

The pupil is asked: "Where did you go this morning?"
"I went to the tablet house," is the answer.
"Did you not play about on the way there?"
"I did not play about."
"And what did you do in the tablet house?"
"First I had to recite my homework. Then I prepared my new tablet. I copied out the text that the supervisor gave me. Then I ate my lunch. After 'Break,' the father of the tablet house asked me questions. Last of all, I was given a written task that I had to do in the tablet house. After my lessons I went straight home. My father heard me recite and was pleased with what I had learned in the tablet house. It was a good school day. But

the next day was not a good one for me. I was late getting up and had no time to eat my breakfast.

" 'Give me two rolls to take with me,' I begged my mother. She gave me two bread rolls and I hurried. All the same, I arrived late.

" 'Why have you come so late?' the monitor asked me. My heart pounded as I stepped before the teacher. I made a deep bow. He forgave me. But when later I went out of the tablet house without permission, the big brother with the stick caned me several times. And when I was caught talking in class, I was caned again. The worst punishment, however, was when the monitor told me 'No one can read that handwriting of yours!' That evening, I complained to my father about my bad marks. And so he invited the father of the tablet house to our house, placed him in the seat of honor, and gave him dinner. He presented him with a jar of oil, a robe, some money, and he placed a ring on his finger as well.

"Then the father of the tablet house spoke with a different voice: 'This son of the tablet house will ascend the highest pinnacles of the art of writing. The day will come when he will be first among his brothers.' "

Several copies of this essay have survived, so obviously the Sumerian teachers were particularly fond of giving it to their pupils as an exercise.

Another text shows that these teachers made an effort to stop their pupils from getting bored at school. They even tried to brighten up arithmetic lessons, as we can tell from one of a number of fables designed to make counting fun. The story is told of a cunning wolf who had to share a kill with nine stupid ones. The wolves, it seems, broke into a sheep pen and made off with ten sheep. Nine of the wolves could not wait to begin tearing them apart, but the tenth wolf, who was very cunning, said: "Fair shares for all. First we must divide them up between us."

"What do you mean, 'fair shares'?" asked the nine wolves who were so greedy to begin that they could not think.

"We shall divide them between us so that the answer is always ten," proposed the sly wolf. "You nine wolves get one sheep and that makes ten for you. I will have nine sheep to myself, and that makes ten as well. That's right, isn't it?"

"Yes, that is right," answered the nine wolves, and they fell upon the one carcass as the cunning wolf pushed it toward them. They were so busy devouring their one sheep that they did not notice how the sly one was dragging away the other nine, one after the other.

Arithmetic disguised as stories must mave been amusing for Sumerian schoolboys, but there is no doubt that a great deal was demanded of them. The script was very complex, although it had developed from clear and unambiguous signs; that is, from pictorial representations of striking objects, reduced to very simplified forms. In Kish, archaeologists found the oldest signs of all engraved on a limestone tablet, showing a head, a foot, and a threshing hammer. For mountains, three peaks were drawn, an arrow stood for an arrow, and a jug for a jug. Many ideas were conveyed by combining two pictures. An "eye" and "water" meant "weep"; "flesh" and a "stick" gave the word "punishment"; "woman" and "jewelry" signified "princess." Many of the signs had several meanings. Thus a locust could mean both the insect and "destruction"; a star could indicate "star" or "heaven" or "god."

Cuneiform, like our own writing, ran from left to right. Originally the signs had been written vertically, but later they were placed horizontally because the scribes found it more comfortable to write that way. They mastered their craft so admirably that a small tablet no bigger than one's hand could be filled with several hundred signs. Once a tablet was covered with writing, it was baked and the text then stood as a record for all time. Important contracts and letters were placed inside an "envelope" on which the scribe wrote the text a second time.

Document and cover were then placed in the kiln together. If there should be any doubt later as to whether the text on the cover was genuine or not, one had only to break it open. Inside lay the original that no one could have tampered with nor altered by a single stroke.

Writing was the greatest of the Sumerians' inventions, and they put it to good use. This is demonstrated by the finds in Nippur and Shuruppak, in Uruk and Ur, and almost all the Sumerian sites. These records consist not only of catalogs and accounts, commands, decrees and laws, but also of astronomical and mathematical texts, of letters and contracts, prayers and incantations, hymns and narrative poems written down by the hundreds.

Clay for such tablets was carefully prepared beforehand. First it was placed in water and stirred thoroughly in order to separate the light from the heavy parts. Stalks, dirt, and leaves floated to the surface and were easily skimmed off. Pebbles sank to the bottom together with other impurities, and the sediment could thus be scraped away leaving behind the pure clay in which the scribe could make his marks, "as if a god were guiding his hand."

The clay tablets of the Sumerians are remarkably durable. Even the unbaked tablets dried only in the sun have lain in the earth for thousands of years without losing their shape. If one takes a stiff brush and removes the earth clinging to a tablet, the cuneiform impressions emerge clearly. And even when the whole is encrusted with salts, the text can often be rescued.

These tablets can be rebaked in a kiln at this late date, and after scrubbing and perhaps treating with acids and boiling water, the inscriptions on them become legible once more.

*Opposite page: Origin and development of eighteen representative cuneiform signs. For their explanation see pp. 315–318 from S. N. Kramer's* History Begins at Sumer, (*Thames & Hudson 1958*)

The worst problems arise, however, when small rodents or earthworms attack the tablets in the ground. Every scholar concerned has had to contend with these destructive vermin, and each has a story to tell about the nuisance they cause. Edward Chiera, in his book *They Wrote on Clay,* mentions the various kinds of damage they have done. Some worms worked their way round the outside of the tablets; others, more enterprising, ate their way clean through the clay, leaving neat holes behind. The most serious inroads were made, however, by the creatures that felt their way across the surface, thereby destroying whole lines of text. By the time they had finished, the tablets looked like the inside of worm-eaten tree bark.

The archaeologists christened these predators "the original bookworms," and they often had hard things to say about them for the havoc they wrought. They played many a trick on the serious scholars who were devoting themselves to the task of deciphering these ancient texts.

# Tricks, Forgeries, and Practical Jokes

The worst tricks played on the excavators in Mesopotamia were the work of Arabs who pitched their tents in the vicinity of the dig. Among them were many tribesmen who were old hands at grave robbing. Many of the tribes regarded the *tells* and all they contained as their personal property and they greeted the explorers with open hostility.

Dr. Robert Koldewey, who dug out the ruins of Babylon and who refused to be driven from his task by the outbreak of World War I, reports in his diaries some of the difficulties he encountered.

For example, the expedition could only fetch essentials such as sugar, flour, salt, lamps, and reed mats if an armed escort were provided. Then there were the endless Arab feuds. Bedouin of the tribe of Beni Hejjem had had some of their sheep stolen, and they decided to search for the missing animals among Koldewey's Arab laborers. This ended in a skirmish and hundreds of shots were fired. The Beni Hejjem lost one man and one gun. One of Koldewey's assistants was brought back to camp shot through the abdomen, and another, named Deibel, was wounded in the upper thigh. Deibel was carried to a watchman's hut and there, with a thick plaster of flour, butter, and salt applied to his wound, he was universally admired as a hero.

One day Koldewey was returning to Babylon after visiting an excavation in Shuruppak. With him were a few of his team and a couple of soldiers. The night was sultry, the darkness sinister, and the horses had to be ridden hard. Suddenly there were shots on their right. Koldewey, who knew all about the tribal feuds in the area, could tell that he and his companions were being mistaken for Muntafiq Arabs, who were such notorious raiders and cattle thieves that they were treated as outlaws by the other tribes. The two soldiers kept shouting: "Asker! Asker!" ("Soldiers! Soldiers!") but that did not stop the attackers from firing away under the cover of night.

Koldewey, without hesitation, rode straight in the direction of the firing. His horse was spattered with shot, and the cook, Abdallah, uttered the most pitiful shrieks and sought cover behind his packhorse. Fortunately, either the riflemen could not shoot straight or else their guns were useless. At any rate no one was hurt. The soldiers rounded up the raiders and delivered them a stern lecture. "Are you owls? Are you jackals? Even if you could not see that this is the Bey of Shuruppak, at least you should have recognized us soldiers. You'll all be clapped in jail for this, depend on it."

But of course nothing happened. And that was all for the best, for any countermove would only have provoked a fresh vendetta, as the Americans had discovered, at great expense, in 1889. They had only been able to obtain a permit to dig in Nippur with the greatest difficulty, and then everything was placed in jeopardy by an outbreak of bitter fighting between the Affedi and the Shammar Bedouin. At first the excavation team refused to be put off by the clashes that took place around the camp. Then one night the Sa'id Arabs, who belonged to the Affedi tribe, attacked the American camp and tried to steal their horses. One young Bedouin was fatally wounded. This triggered off a blood feud between the Americans and the Arabs, and the son of the Affedi Sheikh attacked the American camp without his father's knowledge. The Arabs set fire to the camp and ransacked it completely; the excavation team barely escaped with their lives. All they had left were the finds of the expedition, which had no value at all in Arab eyes. The dig was brought to an abrupt con-

*Above and below: Ur, ziggurat and remains of houses.*
*Following pages: Silver vase of Entemena, Lagash, 3rd millenium* B.C. *(Paris)*
*Bronze head, probably of Sargon, Nineveh, c. 2350* B.C. *(Baghdad)*

clusion. Nevertheless, the Americans returned to Nippur the following year. Meanwhile, the young man who had instigated the raid had died of cholera and his father showed that he could be placated by a worthwhile present of dollars. He even supplied workmen from his own clan.

In the months that followed, some very ancient strata were exposed and nearly seven thousand tablets were found. At the beginning of June, however, the team was driven away by the intense heat, and only one person, the expedition's photographer J. H. Haynes, remained at his post to face the pitiless breath of the desert. Haynes built himself a little fortress of mud bricks, and relying exclusively on his own resources, he went on digging in Nippur for another three years. Among the finds he secured were twenty thousand cuneiform tablets. In February 1896, Haynes came to the end of his strength. He had had to contend with the starkness of the desert, inhabitated only by snakes and jackals, with dust storms and heatwaves sweeping over his fortress. Hunger and thirst, the absence of all companionship, and the renunciation of any kind of comfort eventually led to a nervous breakdown. But before it happened, this one man alone rescued twenty thousand clay tablets which can be seen today in the museums of Philadelphia and Istanbul.

No one could count the number of tablets that strayed into the wrong hands and then disappeared forever. The Arabs who plundered these sites usually threw the tablets away, thinking them to be of no value. Pashas who controlled the area where the excavations were under way, occasionally laid claim to a portion of the finds. And if the excavators failed to take a hint that such tablets could be ransomed against a certain sum of money, the documents were lost forever. Sealstones and cylinder seals made from semiprecious stones were often added to ladies' necklaces instead of going to museum collections.

Sealstones could be imitated relatively easily by skilled gem cutters, and an extensive market in forgeries opened up before long. One amusing story of a forgery was told to Chiera by an antique dealer in Baghdad. In the 1930s there lived a gifted gem cutter named Riza, who was particularly expert in copying cylinder seals of Sumerian and Babylonian origin. It was no secret, but as Riza did not sell these seal copies himself he could never be prosecuted, and the antique dealers were his most reliable friends.

One day, a peasant came to a certain dealer with a cylinder seal of exceptional beauty and he asked a considerable sum for it. The antiquary haggled with him, but when the peasant stuck to his price, the dealer asked him to leave the seal with him for a couple of days so that he could examine it thoroughly and think over the purchase. The peasant was hardly out of the shop before the dealer was off to Riza. And Riza rose to the occasion. He made such a fine copy of the cylinder seal that it was indistinguishable from the original, at least by a peasant. That was clear when the latter reappeared two days later. To his astonishment, two identical objects were held out for his inspection, and the antiquary told him that he could not possibly pay such a high price for a cylinder of which there were duplicates in circulation. As far as the dealer was concerned, the peasant could take the seal away and he handed him back the counterfeit. The peasant was now more eager to sell than ever, and he dropped the price so much that the shopkeeper simply had to buy the seal or it would have looked suspicious.

A little later, an old customer visited the antiquary, who decided to play a joke on this distinguished archaeologist. He showed him the forgery and the scholar was most enthusiastic. Even the high price the dealer named did not deter him. He took away the seal to study it more closely, promising to come back with the money in a few days' time. The dealer intended to own up to his deception when the scholar returned.

But the archaeologist had to leave Baghdad unexpectedly and three weeks later the antiquary received a check from a museum in payment for the forged seal. What could the dealer do but confess his prank to the museum director? So he sent him the

*Demon's head,
fresco from Tel Ghassul,
4th millenium* B.C.
*(after J. Wiesner)*

original seal and asked that the copy be returned. One can imagine the dealer's astonishment when the director informed him that they had carefully compared the two seals, and the original, they insisted, was the one the archaeologist had acquired, so they would not dream of exchanging it for a forgery. And so the dealer was left with the valuable original!

Such sealstones were used in ancient Mesopotamia to "sign" documents. First the scribe placed his own seal on every document he wrote. Then followed the seals of the parties to the transaction, followed by the witnesses in strict order of precedence. Sometimes the last witnesses could hardly find room enough for their seals, which were crowded to the edges of the tablet. Beside each seal the scribe wrote the name and rank of the person concerned. As the seals of the aristocracy were usually the most beautiful, it is their impressions that have pride of place and are the ones best preserved. The impressions made by the seals of humble citizens are, by comparison, often blurred or imperfect.

There were poor people in Sumer at all times, and one story

has survived of a man from Nippur who had little money but plenty of mother wit. It is told in a hundred lines on a cuneiform tablet found hundreds of miles from Nippur by an Anglo-Turkish expedition under Seton Lloyd. It was discovered in the mound of Sultan Tepe together with six hundred other clay tablets that had belonged to the library of a priest. The name of this poor man from Nippur was *Gimilninurta*.

One day, so the story begins, Gimilninurta was sitting at home, lost in gloomy thought. He had no money, no meat, no beer, no bread—there was too much lacking for his liking. He wanted to give a party for his friends, but all he had was a fine cloak. He tried to barter it for a sheep, but it would only buy a goat and he still had not got the beer he needed for a feast. Then Gimilninurta had an idea. He tied a string round the goat's neck and led it to the mayor's house. He would invite the mayor to the feast and perhaps he would then supply the beer. The porter, assuming that the goat was a present for his master, allowed the poor man to come in.

When Gimilninurta mentioned his idea to the mayor, the indignant worthy told his servants to throw the fellow out, but first they should give him a bone, a small draught of beer, and a good thrashing. Gimilninurta was highly offended and swore he would have his revenge three times over. Fortunately for him, the king happened to be in Nippur at that time. To him the rascal went. He kissed his majesty's feet and with persuasive words he begged the king to lend him the state coach, for which he would pay a *mina* of gold. The king was taken aback at the offer, for even a monarch does not turn down a *mina* of gold so lightly. So Gimilninurta borrowed the royal coach and, suitably dressed, drove past the mayor, who stared at him open-mouthed.

Gimilninurta then boasted around that he had deposited a valuable treasure in the temple strong room for which the mayor was responsible. The mayor at once gave a feast, hoping for a share in the treasure. At the banquet, however, he drank more than he should have, and when he lay in a stupor under the table, Gimilninurta pretended there had been an attack on the strong room and his treasure had been stolen. He demanded instant compensation, and the mayor, rapidly sobered, immediately offered him two *minas* of gold. Gimilninurta pocketed the money and, accusing the mayor of dishonesty, gave him a sound beating because honest citizens were deprived of their property through his negligence. At the final blow, Gimilninurta burst out laughing: "That settles the first score!" he declared as he hurried into the royal coach and galloped off to the palace where he returned the coach and handed over the agreed fee. Then as he fingered the other gold *mina* in his pocket, he pondered as to how he would obtain the second installment of his revenge.

He had his head shaved and, disguised as a doctor, he announced himself at the mayor's house as the Miracle Worker from Larsa. There he gabbled off a whole list of illnesses he was sure the mayor was suffering from, and he promised to cure them if he was left alone with the patient in a completely darkened room. Impressed by the "doctor's" confident manner, the mayor agreed, but once in the darkness, Gimilninurta administered his second dose of punishment. The mayor was not laughing this time as the cheeky rascal left the house crowing "That settles the second score!"

The mayor now had watchmen posted, but a week later there was an excited to-do outside his house. A man leading a goat passed by, shouting in a provocative voice: "I am the man with the goat, I am the man with the goat!" The watchmen tried to catch him but he ran away. There was a great hue and cry, with all the household joining in and giving chase. But the real "man-with-the-goat," Gimilninurta, crept into the mayor's house —and for the third time he gave him a good hiding. Satisfied at last, the poor man turned to the chief citizen: "Have I not repaid you handsomely for the beating you gave me, the small beer and the bone?"

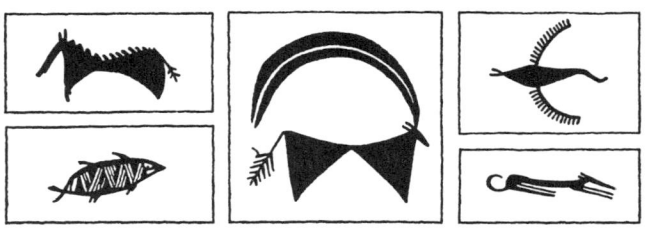

*Paintings on pottery, 5th millenium* B.C. *(after Upham Pope)*

Thus did the rogue, Gimilninurta, have his revenge on the corrupt mayor of Nippur.

There is another story in cuneiform script in which a mayor plays the leading role. It was a mayor of Akkaka who once found himself in a tight corner and all because of a lion. His dilemma is told vividly in a letter discovered in the palace archives in Mari. This is what the mayor writes: "To announce to my lord, thus speaks Yakkim Adad, your servant. It is five days since I sent you a messenger to say that a lion has been captured in a field in Akkaka. My lord should let me know if it is to remain there. If, however, the lion is to be delivered to my lord's palace, will your lordship be good enough to send me instructions to that effect. I wrote to you about this five days ago, but have received no reply. We have already thrown a dog and a pig to the lion. But I keep worrying about what would happen if the lion escaped and did much mischief. In my anxiety, I have lured the lion into a cage and had the cage put on board ship. And now the lion is on the way to my lord."

The mayor was unlikely to have been censured for his decision, for only the king had the right to dispose of lions, to hunt them or have them killed. It is quite possible that the king had this particular lion taken from the cage and put in a zoo. The rulers of ancient Mesopotamia loved to have wild and tame animals and to keep them for show. Tablets and pictures on seals show that Shulgi, for instance, a king of the third dynasty of Ur, had establishments for training animals and extensive wildlife reserves. There were wild cattle and herds of ibex and goat, antelope and gazelle, as well as monkeys and ostriches, onagers and bears. The meat of young bears was a delicacy and they were delivered regularly to the royal kitchens. That from old bears was given to the royal pack of hounds. Bears were also used to guard the city gates, and so were fierce dogs and boars with terrifying tusks. Sumerian and Babylonian zoos had parrots on display as well as many other animals brought to Mesopotamia from distant lands, for the frontiers were open on all sides. The caravan routes led west, east, and north, and to the south lay the broadest highway of all, the sea.

# Uruk and Aratta

Digging in Ur, the archaeologists found beads made of amazonite lying in strata from the days "before the Flood." The nearest source of amazonite is the Nilghiri hills in India. There are Sumerian seals with elephants and rhinoceroses in procession that are so like seals from India that one cannot tell which are which. Carnelian beads etched with Indian patterns were found by Woolley in a king's grave in Ur. The list could be continued indefinitely.

The paths that link India with Mesopotamia are as old as the deserts and mountains that divide them, said the traders in later years. Even in the fourth millennium B.C. sailing ships crossed the sea between the mouths of the Indus and the Euphrates. From December to March, the monsoon blows from east to west and in the following months, from west to east; with the help of these winds even a distance of nearly two thousand miles could be covered.

Two islands, Failaka and Bahrein, lie on this age-old shipping lane and they became important trading stations. Bahrein was known as Dilmun in the old days and the Sumerians called it the "Great Fish in the Eastern Sea." They believed that it had not always stood where it does, but that originally it had risen from the sea off the Indian coast, and with its weird inhabitants, half-human, half-fish, it had floated westward. These creatures had gone ashore at Eridu and settled in the Land of Ur. Enki, the god of the watery deeps, had given this island his special blessing and for several thousand years Dilmun belonged to the old Mesopotamian empire.

During excavations on the island, a large settlement was found. It already had a temple in the third millennium B.C. and its layout was Sumerian, although there were also features in Indian style. One trench in the temple area contained pearls, amulets, lapis lazuli, and copper votive gifts. The figure of a "worshiper," seventeen cylinder seals, and a bull's head of bronze resembled strongly those from the king's graves at Ur. On the other hand, eight seals were similar to those of ancient India, and the most striking association of all was a pond with steps leading to it, which had been built into the temple terrace. Pools like this were a common feature in temples in the Far East, countries which, according to tradition, Enki loved best next to Sumer.

Ships sailed south from Eridu, Ur, and other Sumerian harbors, and they went as far as the east coast of Africa. Excavations in Amarna, Egypt, where Ikhnaton built his palace, produced numerous Mesopotamian seals and cylinder seals and many cuneiform tablets. The Sumerians brought diorite from Nubia, Arabia, and east Africa, from Egypt they imported gold, and copper came from Cyprus. The cedars of Lebanon were transported either by river or overland along the caravan routes. Silver came from the Taurus mountains and asphalt from various sources.

These goods were bartered for wool and textiles, cosmetics and jewelry, oil and corn. The exchange of cereals against lapis lazuli and other semiprecious stones is mentioned frequently. Foreigners came to live in Sumer, too, as we know from the picture of a Pharaoh sketched on one tablet by an Egyptian resident in Mesopotamia.

Even in prehistoric times, the mountains were never an insuperable obstacle to communications. This is clear from an epic poem to which Professor Kramer gave the title *Enmerkar and the Lord of Aratta*. According to the old king-lists, Enmerkar belonged to the first dynasty of Uruk, as did Gilgamesh. He was the son of the sun-god Utu, who founded Uruk and first invented writing.

Kramer discovered this long epic on a clay tablet about nine inches square, or roughly the size of a sheet of typewriting paper. The Sumerian scribe had squeezed more than six hundred signs on it. With the help of another twenty tablets and various fragments, most of the text was recovered. This is the story:

When Enmerkar was king of Uruk, a proud king ruled in Aratta, a city far to the east. Aratta was rich in copper, silver, and gold as well as in semiprecious stones. Seven mountain ranges lay between Aratta and Uruk, but Enmerkar, who wished to decorate the shrine of Inanna with precious metals and stones, sent a herald to the lord of Aratta to proclaim the following message: "The lord of Uruk, Enmerkar the son of the sun-god Utu, has sent me to you. His messenger has crossed seven mountains in order to make known to you his will. Tell the people of Aratta to bring stone down from the mountains to the valley so that a fairer temple for Inanna may be built in Uruk. They shall fashion the silver and gold into holy vessels. Lapis lazuli and carnelian shall they quarry from the mountain sides so that the house of Inanna may gleam with rich adornment. Let them fill panniers with the precious burdens and secure them to the backs of mountain asses. The shrine of Inanna shall they adorn and they shall kneel before the sanctuary like mountain sheep. But if you refuse to do this, then Enki's curse will strike you and your city. The lord of Uruk will come and drive the inhabitants of Aratta before him, so that they flee like startled birds into a nest nearby. Inanna herself will take arms to subdue Aratta and heap dust upon the city."

Then spoke the lord of Aratta. "How can that be? Inanna's temple, so rich in treasure, is here, is it not? Has not Inanna enthroned me as lord of Aratta, so that I may lock the gates of the mountains?"

"The days when Inanna dwelt in Aratta are over," answered the herald. "Now she has her dwelling in Uruk and she demands the riches of Aratta."

Then the lord of Aratta was frightened and said: "If Inanna has become my enemy then I will meet the lord of Uruk with weapons. But if he will send me corn, he shall receive silver and carnelian in return."

With this message, the herald returned to Uruk. Enmerkar consulted Nidaba, the goddess of wisdom, had a caravan of asses laden with corn and sent the messenger to Aratta for the second time. But he also gave him his scepter to take with him. The corn was piled high in the marketplace of Aratta and the people rejoiced and clamored for their king to send the jewels in exchange. But although the scepter of the king of Uruk filled the lord of Aratta with alarm, he proposed to settle the dispute by single combat, wherein the Sumerian champion should be clad in a garment that was neither black nor white, neither brown nor yellow nor checkered. The lord of Aratta informed the king of Uruk that he looked forward to the duel with confidence, for Inanna had in no wise abandoned her house in Aratta for good.

The end of the tale is missing but another account of the dispute tells us something of the outcome. A certain priest came to the assistance of the lord of Aratta. He offered to stride across the two rivers, to conquer all the lands from the sea to the cedar mountains and to return to Aratta with ships laden to the brim. Highly delighted, the lord of Aratta fitted out the priest and he went forth to Uruk. Through his magic, he was able to destroy all the livestock of Uruk in their stalls and sheep pens, and the shepherds fled. But now the servants of Nidaba rose against the priest, and they outwitted him so that his face grew black with anger. He met his death in the waters of the Euphrates, and instead of returning to Aratta with ships heaped high with spoils, he floated out to sea like a spar of driftwood. When the lord of Aratta heard the news, he hurriedly sent a herald to Enmerkar with this message: "You are the one chosen by Inanna and yours alone is the kingship. You are the lord of the upper and lower lands and I yield precedence to you. From my birth, I have not been your equal, you are the big brother and I cannot compare myself with you." And so, after the long-drawn-out quarrel, the lord of Uruk won. Inanna received the gold and silver, lapis lazuli and carnelian for her temple which was transferred to Uruk, and she abandoned Aratta forever.

The true meaning of this story is that at some time or other, Inanna migrated westward, like the "fish-people" who came from the east to found a new homeland in the plains between the two rivers. It comes as no surprise that the Sumerians wrote the word for "land" with a sign that was made of three mountain tops standing side by side, the same as that for a mountain range. For their old homeland lay "beyond the mountains." We know for certain that the Sumerians came from the east, although even today, no one is certain when this happened.

The deeper the archaeologists dig into the soil of Mesopotamia, the more astonishing are their finds. They come upon the remains of temples, jewelry, and vessels which could only have belonged to some pre-Sumerian culture. Probably the immigrants came from the east, and found even then an established community with a higher degree of development in architecture, pottery, canal building, and administration than their own. Certainly the Sumerians caught up with them quickly and soon overtook them. The invention of writing is undoubtedly their achievement, for the word "man" is an unmistakably Sumerian head. And it was the Sumerians who first made the Land of the Two Rivers into a paradise.

A number of Sumerian cities challenged each other for precedence, notably Kish and Uruk, Ur and Nippur, Lagash and Umma; and the rivalry was not always peaceful but sometimes led to war. Even solemnly binding treaties were broken if princes thought it was to their advantage to do so. The soil grew so fertile that every square foot became precious, and battles were fought over a single field. Then the patron gods of the cities joined in, and they decided the issues of victory and defeat.

# The Quarrel over the Garden of Eden

Twenty-five miles northeast of Uruk, and forty-five north of Ur lies the mound of Telloh. It was here, in 1877, that the French archaeologist Ernest de Sarzec began his excavations. He dug there for many seasons and he uncovered the first Sumerian city, Lagash. But even as late as 1889, a world-famous scholar could deny the very existence of the Sumerians. In his *Assyrian Grammar* he wrote: "The Semitic Babylonians were right when they attributed the invention of writing to their god Nabu. And as there are no references anywhere in Babylonian texts to a third race coexisting with themselves and the Kassites, this can be explained once and for all by the simple fact that no such people as the Sumerian-Akkadians ever existed."

Year after year, Sarzec unearthed statues, reliefs, seals, and clay tablets of Sumerian origin from the hill that he had made his own special field of discovery. Thanks to these and later finds, we know more about Lagash and its history than about the fates of other Sumerian cities such as Uruk, Ur, and Eridu.

In January 1872, as soon as Sarzec took up the post of French consul in Basra, he started looking for likely sites that were worth investigating for evidence of buried civilizations. A merchant named Asfar gave him a tip. There were, he said, remains of clay tablets and ruins of statues, some of them very big ones, strewn over the mound of Telloh. This was within the territory of the Muntafiq Bedouin, who were apt to greet every foreigner with suspicion, and as often as not, with well-aimed gunfire, too.

Very diplomatically, Sarzec was able to gain both the confidence and the protection of Nasir Pasha, the tribe's principal chief. This achieved, the consul set out for the north, without any exaggerated hopes, however. But as he wandered over the hill, he found remains at every step and turn, potsherds, clay tablets, and fragments of carvings and statues lying about in the open. What riveted his attention most was part of a colossal statue of diorite, with an inscription engraved on one shoulder. It lay at the foot of a hill and the rain and the wind had already freed it from the surrounding earth. Ernest de Sarzec decided to start work immediately.

A word from Nasir Pasha procured for him the workmen he needed. He lined them up in a row and then had them dig deep trenches right through the mound. From March 1877 onward, he combed the site methodically. It had lain undisturbed for many centuries and finds came to light in undreamed of quantities. The dig went on until the middle of June, and then the workmen went on strike because the ground grew burning hot beneath the gaze of the sun.

In February 1878, Sarzec was back in the field again and once more the work went on till June. A walled terrace on which a temple had once stood emerged from the rubble, as well as the lower portion of the diorite statue Sarzec had found at his first inspection. It was so heavy that it had to be covered over again very carefully and left inside the mound for the time being. Sarzec did this apprehensively, for rumors of the abundant finds in Telloh had spread as far as Nineveh, Baghdad, and Istanbul, and Sarzec had reason to fear that Hormuzd Rassam might get his grasping hands on the statue and send it to England. The artful Rassam, with his incomparable "excavator's luck" did indeed turn up at Telloh, but he failed in his attempt to acquire the statue, which reached the Louvre successfully. By that time it was complete, for Sarzec had been fortunate enough to find the head as well.

Advised by experts, Sarzec extracted so many finds from Tel-

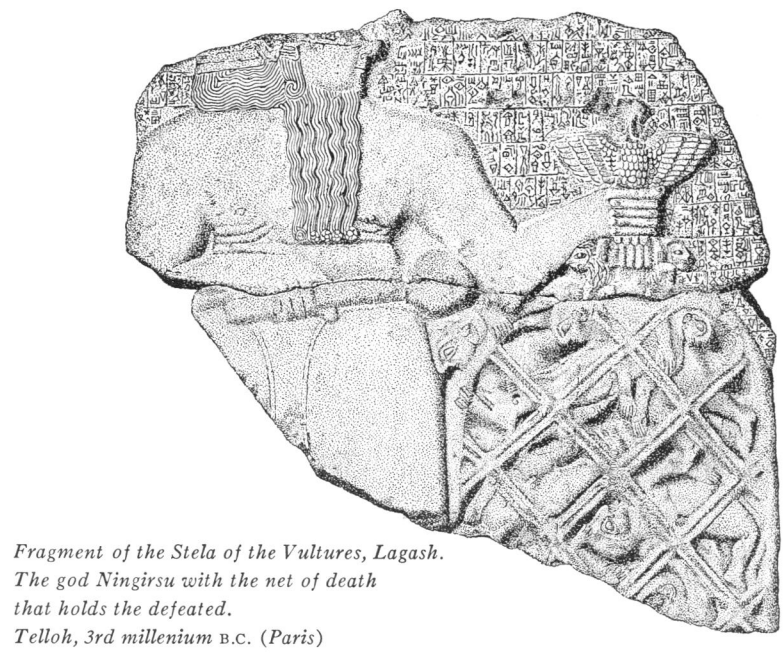

*Fragment of the Stela of the Vultures, Lagash.
The god Ningirsu with the net of death
that holds the defeated.
Telloh, 3rd millenium B.C. (Paris)*

loh that he is ranked as one of the foremost archaeologists. Apart from works of art, he discovered many inscribed barrel-shaped monuments and cylinders of the greatest importance, and approximately forty thousand inscribed tablets.

Sarzec had his young wife with him and she proved a most able assistant, her husband's equal both in bravery and stamina. With her by his side he defied all the difficulties. He was not deterred by sandstorms or cloudbursts, by raiders, illness or intrigue. In the end, he managed to gain the good will of the sultan in Constantinople, which stopped him from being seriously molested by the Arabs during his later excavations. He was also able to uncover a number of temples and palaces.

Among his more important finds must be mentioned seven statues of the city's king, Gudea; a silver vase belonging to King

Entemena and a battle club inscribed with the name of King Mesilim of Kish. There were also the remains of a limestone stela, on which there is an excellent description of a battle, side by side with impressive illustrations. It may be called "The Quarrel over the Garden of Eden" for it concerns a strip of boundary land of that name. One fragment of this stela had already been found at the first excavation. It shows vultures fighting for human flesh, the heads and arms of dismembered soldiers. The block is about five feet high and it is known as The Stela of the Vultures after the piece first discovered. It was a monument to commemorate the victory of the god of Lagash, Ningirsu, and the city's king, Eannatum.

This king belonged to the dynasty that was founded by Mesannepada about 2500 B.C. At that time Mesilim was king of Nippur and Kish and he considered himself the lord over the whole of Sumer. When a quarrel broke out between the cities of Umma and Lagash about a strip of land at the common frontier, Mesilim intervened as arbitrator. He consulted the gods, and they declared that the disputed stretch was beloved by Ningirsu, that is, it belonged to Lagash. Mesilim dug a demarcation ditch, set up a boundary stone, and sent the enemy armies home again. But as soon as Ush became lord of Umma, he uprooted the boundary stone, filled in the ditch, and occupied the Garden of Eden.

Lagash did not take that lying down. Its king was Eannatum, a great warrior who had already extended his dominion over several neighboring cities, and he led his troops against the army of Umma. A battle took place in the Garden of Eden and the gods fought on both sides, with no less than seven befriending Lagash. They threw their battle nets over the invaders from Umma, which meant death for many of them. The rest fled. Eannatum forbade his soldiers to pursue the beaten army. He also refrained from laying waste their fields. He himself received a spear wound, and his god shed tears at the sight of it.

In a new treaty, the Garden of Eden was awarded for the

second time to Lagash. A boundary canal was dug down to groundwater level, and a boundary stone was set. As the victor had behaved with such restraint, peace was secured for the immediate future.

The Stela of the Vultures tells the story of the great event in words and pictures. On the back, the battle itself is shown, from the point of view of Eannatum and his soldiers. With lances lowered, the Lagash infantry attacks, protected by leather shields and helmets. The king, who is only a little taller than his men, is leading them. He wears a thick sheepskin thrown over one shoulder. In his right hand he holds a curved scimitar. The field is strewn with his slain foes. A second attack is led by the king from his war chariot. He flings a javelin which pierces the head of one of the enemy's soldiers. The king's hair streams out from beneath his helmet. The fallen soldiers from the ranks of Lagash are given a solemn burial. Men carry earth in baskets, an ox lies ready to be sacrificed. The enemy dead are left to the vultures and the prisoners are led into slavery, which has been the custom as long as men have made war on one another.

The front panel of the stela is reserved for the gods. By their intervention they have decided the victory shall go to Lagash. Ningirsu, the patron god of the city dominates the battlefield. The knot of hair at the back of his head has come loose like the king's. This indicates the feverish excitement of the conflict. His glance spreads terror, his mouth is like a knife. His right hand grasps the handle of a club and his left grips the battle net in which the conquered enemies flounder like fish. The net is fastened by a lion-headed eagle clutching two lions. There is no escape for the men trapped inside the net.

It seems as if the god was less merciful than the king. For in order to prevent any future clashes, Eannatum laid out a strip of no-man's-land as a buffer between the two states. He even allowed the men of Umma to go on tilling the soil of the Garden of Eden, on condition that they handed over part of the produce to Lagash. By this decision he not only avoided humiliating the

*Stone tablet with the symbols of the god Ningirsu, 3rd millenium* B.C., *Telloh (Paris)*

defeated people, but also obtained considerable supplies for his own city. Most of all, he showed he was an experienced general, for having secured his rear, he could now advance farther to the east and the north. Eannatum conquered both Nippur and Kish, and in the end, he called himself the king of the whole of Sumer.

Entemena, the nephew and next to the last successor to Eannatum, has recorded the sequel to the above events. On one clay "barrel" the story is told of how peace between Lagash and Umma was shattered once again, when a new king of Umma rebelled against Lagash. He diverted water from the boundary canal and overturned the stela. Entemena called him a plunderer of fields and farms, a man with an evil tongue, and he won a victory over him. The defeated king fled, leaving sixty corpses in the ditch and five mounds of the slain in five different villages. For the third time the boundary was restored where Mesilim, king of Kish, had drawn it.

Entemena who, like Eannatum, was led to victory by the city god Ningirsu "dug out the great canal that, at the word of Enlil, may not be altered. He built a firm foundation for the canal and he restored it for Ningirsu, his lord whom he loved, and for the patron goddess of the city did he make the restoration."

Entemena, king of Lagash, was presented with the scepter of Sumer by Enlil and endowed with the wisdom of Enlil. That is how the story reads on the clay tablet. It closes with this threat: "Should any man of Umma cross the canal of the god Ningirsu in order to take possession of a field, or should a man of the mountain do so, may Enlil strike him." Later records tell us that for a long time there was no lasting peace between the Sumerian cities. It was an age when the city princes were consumed with ambition to become "Lord over the whole land from the upper sea to the lower sea." It is true that even on the battlefield, so they insist on their monuments, they are fighting in the service of the gods. But their deeds give the impression that the gods were important to them only as their allies in war. It was a long time since kings had been content to live within the temple precincts. They had built themselves palaces with stout walls instead. Their mistrust was mutual and each ruler wracked his brains to think of a way of diverting another city's water supplies for his own use.

# A King of the Oppressed

The Sumerians looked up to their early kings as though they were the sons of gods. The kings of the first dynasties after the Flood were also "the cultivators of meadows, tamers of the wild rivers, subduers of beasts of prey," who offered sacrifices and conferred with the gods on all important questions, so that the "Land of the Black-headed People" should be well ruled. The king combined the offices of monarch and high priest, and the priesthood helped him to carry out his duties. On his behalf they controlled the taxes and the produce of the harvests; they were responsible for work in the fields, along the canals, and in the workshops; and they laid down the penalties for any shortcomings or failure to perform one's duty. For it was considered a sin, that is, an offense against the divine order of things, if someone was lazy, or secretly obtained an advantage at someone else's expense. The priests distributed the new "lots," that is they decided which field would be allocated to whom for cultivation, and they threatened the disobedient with terrible punishments, the most dire of which would be inflicted after death. All this they did in the name of the king.

But when, as time went by, the city kings were more and more likely to be found at the head of their troops than in the midst of their priests, the most eminent of the priests took the king's place inside the temple. And as the whole machinery of government depended on the priests for its smooth running, the high priests won ever-increasing power over the people. He and the king became rivals. The high priest, too, made his house into a fortress and ensconced himself behind thick walls. The importance of religion receded further and further into the background. What concerned the priests now was how to win as much power as possible over the people. They wanted to squeeze out the king and to rule themselves.

In Lagash, they achieved their object soon after Entemena's siege of the Garden of Eden. When Entemena's son died after only a brief reign, two high priests in succession ascended the throne. The second of them actually bequeathed the kingdom to his son, Lugulanda, whose avarice was so great that he even took personal possession of the fields belonging to the temple. His wife owned land herself, she dealt in corn and cattle, timber and jewelry, and transacted business with other princesses, exchanging gifts with the queen of Adab.

The attempts to grab more and more property often tempted these high officials into committing open injustices, and the priests began to abuse their office. The rich grew even richer and the poor grew poorer. A dangerous and widening rift developed that cut right across the nation. Such was the situation in Lagash from about the year 2370 B.C. onward. The oppressed people waited for a liberator, and a man of the people, Urukagina, appeared and placed himself at the head of the dispossessed. Lugulanda was deposed after nine years on the throne. Of his sons, whose names are mentioned in the records, nothing more is heard. Urukagina drove out the oppressors and re-established order.

Ernest de Sarzec discovered four tablets recording Urukagina's deeds written by contemporary historians at his first dig in Lagash. "At the beginning of time," they say, "the boatmen lived by their boats, the herdsmen by their donkeys and sheep, the fishermen by their fishponds, all in good order," for everything belonged to the patron god of the city, Ningirsu, and to the goddess Baba. But then the priests became overseers and they seized the boats, the cattle, and the fishponds. Outrageous taxes were introduced for everyone and on everything. Now if a man had a sheep sheared and the wool were white, he had to pay a five-shekel shearing tax. If a man divorced his wife, he had to place his five shekels on the table likewise, as divorce tax. If a perfumer prepared toilet oil, he had to pay five shekels tax when he sold it, and an additional fee of one shekel to the chief overseer. When a man died and was buried, the priest took delivery of seven jugs of beer, four hundred and twenty rolls of bread and one hundred and twenty liters of corn liquor. Priests and rich men, whom the priests favored, forced the poor to sell their donkey foals, or even their houses, for a ridiculously low sum. Those in power did not hesitate even to use the oxen of the god Ningirsu to water their own fields. The harvest from the good fields of the god was hoarded in private barns. The high priests took for their own use the best fields for growing onions and cucumbers. In the smaller villages, the priests either confiscated the fruit trees of the poor outright, or made them deliver the gathered fruit. The people were subdued by threats.

Urukagina took drastic action. He abolished serfdom and he restored freedom. In one document, in which the building of a canal and reservoir are attributed to Urukagina, these words appear:

When Ningirsu, Enlil's successor, gave the kingship to Urukagina, whose hand he grasped from among the thirty-six thousand people in the city, this king restored freedom once more and obeyed the commands that Ningirsu gave him. He liberated the boatmen and the shepherds, the herdsmen and the fishermen from those who had seized the control of boats and herds and ponds. The unnecessary overseers were removed from the storehouses, and the tax collectors from the villages. A man who had a sheep sheared need pay no more shearing tax, even if the wool were white; whoever prepared perfumed oil and sold it need no longer pay the oil tax. When a dead man was buried, the surviving kin need pay the priest only three jugs of beer instead of seven, and only eighty rolls of bread instead of four hundred and twenty, and for the religious service, the payment expected

*Sumerian musician, terra-cotta relief, c. 1900 B.C. (Chicago)*

would be at most a young goat, or perhaps a bed. No priest might any longer force his way into the garden of a poor man. If a poor man's donkey foaled and the rich man wanted to defraud the owner by buying it for a ridiculous sum, the poor man could now say "I want so-and-so much for it," and he would be given what seemed to him a fair price in good coin.

Urukagina made a bond with Ningirsu in which he pledged himself to protect widows and orphans from the powerful. He drove out the overseers, so that there were no more exploiters in the whole land as far as the sea. He freed the children of Lagash from the threat of usury, theft, and murder, and with Ningirsu's help, he also rid the land of drought. He himself returned to Ningirsu all the fields and houses that had come into the king's personal domains. And like the kings in the old days, he was once more prince and priest combined, and *ensi*, or governor, who ruled at the god's behest.

After restoring order in Lagash, Urukagina had to defend it

at the frontiers, especially against the princes of Umma who persisted in deeds of violence even in the strip of no-man's-land. Like Eannatum and Entemena, Urukagina also repelled the aggressors. On one occasion he inflicted on them such great losses that the defeat caused a revolution in Umma—to the destruction of Lagash. For now a great warrior came to the fore in Umma. His name was Lugalzaggisi.

Lugalzaggisi dreamed of bringing all the cities of Sumer under his dominion and extending the frontiers of his empire beyond the rivers as far as the upper and lower seas. He raised an army and he put it through a rigorous training program. Then he attacked Lagash. Urukagina was killed and his army was defeated. One eyewitness lamented the destruction of Lagash. He gives a vivid description of the "seven and thirty" deeds of violence committed at the instigation of Lugalzaggisi.

The people of Umma have set fire to the shrine of Ningirsu. They have taken away the adornment of the temple, gold and silver and precious stones. In the palace of the king, in the temple of Enlil, in the temple of Baba they have shed blood. They have overturned the altars and broken the statues. They have taken the ripe corn from the fields of Ningirsu. When the people of Umma destroyed Lagash, they tainted themselves with a sin. The power they have seized for themselves by such a crime they will lose again. It was not Urukagina, the king of Lagash, who upset the divine order. It was Lugalzaggisi, the king of Umma, who has broken the laws of the gods. May he be torn to pieces for it. And may his goddess, Nisaba, carry these sins on her own head.

This lament is both a condemnation and a curse, which was to be fulfilled, although not until a quarter of a century later.

At first the power of Umma increased. Lugalzaggisi led his troops from victory to victory. The conquered cities were made to supply soldiers for the wars of aggression that followed. When Uruk had fallen into his hands, he built a new palace within the walls of Gilgamesh. From Uruk he marched on Ur, on Larsa, on

Shuruppak, and Kish. Nippur fell to him, too, and with it the kingship of the whole of Sumer. He advanced south toward the sea and captured Eridu. He stormed up the Euphrates and conquered Mari. Then he marched his soldiers, "numerous as weeds," as far as the Mediterranean coast, the first Sumerian king to advance so far to the west.

When his battles were over, he set about administering the lands that were now his, but Lagash was the one city for which he had nothing but hatred until the end of his days. On one valuable vase, the conquering hero proclaimed his deeds in war and in peace:

Lugalzaggisi, inspired by the gods, chosen by Enlil for the kingship over the whole of Sumer, subdued the lands from the rising to the setting sun. He smoothed the ways for the god from the lower to the upper sea. He made the people dwell in safety and he watered the land with the waters of joy. To the god of the skies, Anu, he addressed the following prayer: "Add life to my life and let the Land of Sumer blossom. Let the breasts of heaven overflow! Let the good fate that the gods have ordained for me remain mine forever. Let me remain always as the shepherd at the head of my flock!"

Anu did not listen to this prayer of Lugalzaggisi's. The Sumerians did not regard him as a king of their own, because he had conquered them with the same ruthlessness he had used to subdue the Amorites in the west or the Subartu in the mountains. After "the man from Umma" had reigned for twenty-five years, he was defeated by one who had risen from the Euphrates. He called himself Sargon: that is, the rightful king. He shattered Lugalzaggisi's army, took him prisoner, and placed him on display in a cage like a wild beast in front of the shrine of Enlil in Nippur.

This conqueror was a Semite. None of the Sumerian royal cities was good enough to be the capital of his kingdom. So he built himself a new city and called it Akkad.

# Akkad, the New City

In 1931, the British archaeologist R. Campbell Thompson was digging in the hill of Kuyunjik. He came upon a copper head that was at least fifteen hundred years older than the lion-hunt reliefs and clay tablets of Ashurbanipal discovered by Layard in the nineteenth century. This head may very well be a likeness of King Sargon. There is a certain majesty about the face. The hair is artistically arranged, gathered into a knot at the back and kept in place by a firm headband. Arched eyebrows curve like birds' wings above the empty eye sockets, the left one of which has been slashed into an ugly jagged hole. The nose protrudes boldly and an arrogant smile plays about the full mouth framed by an elaborately curled and barbered beard. The expression shows both shrewdness and ruthlessness. Strength of will and dignity have found a perfect combination. The eyes have been gouged out, but the gaze is only the more penetrating for the mutilation. Surely the blow that destroyed the left eye was dealt by some embittered enemy, determined to strike Sargon in effigy and do him an injury even after death.

Thompson, who discovered it, believed that the statue, of which this head was once part, had been carried off to Susa by the victorious Elamites, there mutilated and beheaded, and many centuries later brought back to Nineveh by Ashurbanipal with many other spoils of war.

Sargon had risen from obscurity to become "lord of the four quarters of the earth." His career seemed to his contemporaries and to subsequent generations to be so remarkable that very soon he became a hero of legend. His deeds are recorded in royal inscriptions and chronicles. Even the soothsayers invoked him in their texts. His astonishing rise to power is recorded in the first person on a diorite block, and the mighty man informs the world as follows:

Sargon the great king, king of Akkad, am I. Of my father I know only his name. He was called La'ipu. Otherwise I know nothing of him. My father's brother lived in the mountains. My mother was a priestess whom no man should have possessed. She brought me into the world secretly in the town of Azupirana. She took a basket of reeds, placed me inside it, covered it with pitch, and placed me in the Euphrates. And the river, without which the land cannot live, carried me through part of my future kingdom. The river did not ride over me, but carried me high and bore me along to Akki, who fetched water to irrigate the fields. Akki made a gardener of me. In the garden that I cultivated Inanna saw me. And she turned her favor toward me and promised to make me great. She took me to Kish to the court of King Urzubaba. There I called myself Sargon: that is, the rightful king.

Sargon said nothing about the way he had risen to become the "rightful king." Probably he deposed Urzubaba one day and placed himself on the throne. Then, as he was stronger than all others, he carried them with him. After so many Sumerian kings, he thought it was high time that a Semite ruled the land, for half of its inhabitants were Semites.

When Sargon became king of Kish, Sumer was still in the hands of Lugalzaggisi, who ruled like a tyrant. Sargon accused him of insulting ambassadors from Kish in the palace of Uruk and declared war on him.

Sargon was an able general. His soldiers were well equipped and he had them specially trained for hand-to-hand fighting. He discarded their heavy shields and gave them instead throwing spears, scimitars, and bows. And he kindled their fighting spirit.

This was how he managed to defeat the Sumerian army and throw his net over Lugalzaggisi. When he displayed the vanquished king like a circus beast before the temple of Enlil in Nippur, he broke the pride of the Sumerians. The Black-headed People accepted Sargon as a scourge sent by Enlil to punish them and to rule the whole land.

And now Sargon conquered one city after another, and occupied the land as far as the coast. At Eridu, he washed the blood from his weapons in the sea to signify that from then on there should be peace in Sumer. In order to show that it was not thanks to Enlil or any other Sumerian god that he had risen to be king, but by virtue of his own strength, he chose neither Nippur nor Kish, neither Ur nor Uruk, to be his Capital. He built a new city and he called it Akkad.

For his "house-god" he picked Utu, the sun-god, who reigned in the neighboring city of Sippar. The saw of the sun-god became Sargon's emblem. Like Utu, who rises every morning, radiating light over the world, so Sargon had broken out of the darkness of obscurity and by his victory over the Sumerians, had made a glorious name for himself.

He was determined to rise higher still. First he turned toward the east, to Elam. This was the land through which the Sumerians had once passed on their way to Mesopotamia, the country where Susa and other ancient cities flourished. There stood temples and workshops of high repute, in which potters, smiths, weavers, and sculptors were producing goods as fine as those of Sumer. Sargon made a two-pronged attack on Elam, advancing part of his army along winding mountain paths, while the rest approached from the sea, and thus he defeated the Elamites.

He also occupied the island of Dilmun. Then he marched north to the land of Subartu and he forced the mountain people to acknowledge his sovereignty before returning to Akkad with many prisoners and rich spoils. After a rising against him, he had many villages so ruthlessly exterminated that "even the birds could find no place to build their nests." Finally he attacked the land of the Amorites in the west. There lay the

Taurus Mountains rich in metals. There stretched Lebanon, covered with cedar trees. Sargon marched up the Euphrates and through the land of Mari. He crossed the Silver Mountains, and he conquered the whole land as far as the shores of the Mediterranean Sea.

Now he possessed a kingdom like none before him. He was the mightiest man of his age. Fifty-four hundred men dined every day before his throne, an army tested and tried in many battles. He made especially favored servants into "sons of the palace." They were given posts in all the cities and ruled the land in Sargon's name.

Sargon was a stern ruler who allowed no one to encroach on his power. The Semites had lived side by side with the Sumerians long enough for them to appreciate their high achievements. In many ways they became the pupils of the people they had defeated, taking pains to see that nothing Sumerian was lost.

The kingdom was now called Sumer-Akkad, and Sargon assumed, among others, the titles of the Sumerian kings. He called himself the "king of Akkad and Kish, priest of Anu, viceroy of Inanna, the chosen of Enlil."

"And from the north sea to the south sea, no rival was given him by Enlil." This was inscribed on a diorite block extolling Sargon's achievements. But he felt he owed nothing to any Sumerian god. He was himself "the god of Akkad," strong enough to carry the burden of world sovereignty on his own shoulders.

Sargon reigned for fifty-five years. Toward the end of his life there were rebellions, notably in Elam, Subartu, and Amor. When Sargon died, the nations round Akkad believed that the hour of freedom had struck and there were more revolts. Sargon's son put down the rebels, but after reigning for nine years he was murdered and succeeded by his brother. Something of Sargon's greatness was restored by his grandson, Naramsin. Economy and trade flourished once more in all the lands under his rule, particularly in Akkad and Sumer. It is from this period that we date buildings and sculptures that are unrivaled, but a restless spirit pervaded the age. Many monuments were erected at the frontiers, where battles were fought, instead of being placed in temples. Indeed, so far the archaeologists have failed to find a single temple built by the Akkadians. On the contrary, the Akkadian palaces which have been discovered were built on the foundations of former temples.

The most amazing Akkadian citadel lies far to the north in Tell Brak. The big square bricks from which the walls were built are stamped with the name of Naramsin. The walls were more than thirty-three feet thick. They enclosed a big square courtyard, whose sides are over one hundred and thirty feet long, five smaller courtyards and a number of storerooms. There was only one gate, and this was guarded by turrets. In this fortress, a small troop of men could defy an imposing army.

One can be sure that it was no accident that Naramsin chose a former temple site to build his palace, for his fortress was a temple in itself, dedicated to himself as the god of the kingdom. On the stelae erected in his honor, Naramsin always wore the horned crown, the distinguishing symbol of a god. He called himself "lord of the four quarters of the earth, strong man and hero." Everywhere he had monuments set up to glorify himself, for he won victories in all the surrounding countries. Even deep in Kurdistan a monument was found in honor of Naramsin.

A team of French archaeologists found the most splendid stela to Naramsin, so far discovered, in Susa. Originally it had been erected in Sippar, but one thousand years later the conquering Elamites took it back to their capital with them. It is of reddish sandstone, and the sculptor has left the block almost in its natural shape. There are only fifteen figures chiseled over the smooth front, yet they are distributed so skillfully over the surface area that it conveys the impression of two armies clashing on the battlefield.

Naramsin, with the horned crown on his head, towers over the rest, with battle-axe, bow, and javelin in his hands, and one foot planted on the body of a fallen enemy as on a step. Before him towers a mountain peak, over which stand three suns. One of the foe has been run through by the king's lance, a second is pleading for his life. Others are toppling over a precipice, or are trying to escape. The warriors bear down on the ranks of the enemy like a thunderstorm. No one stood a chance against an attack of such force.

The mountain dwellers of Iran and Taurus were not the only ones to discover this to their cost. Naramsin pressed on as far as Magana and Melukhkha, and invaded Egypt and Nubia so that he could exploit the lands of gold and porphyry. It was through these expeditions in particular that Naramsin, like Sargon before him, became a legendary hero.

Naramsin was the last of the Akkadian rulers who could hold the empire together. When he died, the strength of his people was sapped by their many wars. His son did indeed lay claim to the title Sharkalisharri, which means "king of kings," but he had to defend himself continually against attacks from all sides. And he was succeeded by so many short-lived occupants of the throne that the chronicler of the king-lists asks: "Who was king? Who was not king?" The empire of the Akkadians was ripe for dissolution.

Its destroyers came from the north, from the Zagros mountains. They were the Guti, a half-savage people to whom temples and statues meant nothing. Sargon and Naramsin had kept them at bay by brute force, but now the "dragon from the mountains" invaded the Land of the Two Rivers with fire and destruction. Uruk, Ur, Kish, and Lagash were all conquered. The Akkadians and Sumerians were defeated so crushingly that a whole century passed before they could rise again and shake off the tyranny of the Guti.

According to many of the tablets, the Sumerians felt that this terrible experience was the punishment of the gods, like the Flood. In one collection of inscriptions, which is housed at Jena today, Professor Kramer found a long poem describing these events and their background. In this "Curse of Akkad," Naramsin is blamed for the evil that befell the country.

"He attacked Nippur, the city of Enlil," so it says on the tablets. "And Enlil, whose shrine was desecrated, rose up and called on the avengers, just as he had summoned the Akkadians when the Sumerians had been negligent in his service. At that time, Enlil, like the Bull of Heaven, like a mighty ox, had trampled Uruk in the dust and to Sargon, king of Akkad, he had granted dominion. Akkad had grown rich because Inanna so wished it. The storehouses of Akkad had been filled with gold and silver, copper, tin and lapis lazuli, timber and corn."

It was a good time for children because the land dwelt in peace. Many people brought tribute to Akkad; the Martu from the west, who grew no crops, brought oxen and sheep; the Melukhaites sent ambassadors from the Black Land with ivory. There came Elamites and Subareans, laden like beasts of burden; chieftains and princes from all nations brought gifts, especially at New Year. Thus it was until Naramsin decided to attack the shrine of Enlil. He sent soldiers into the sacred grove of the god to plunder it. They destroyed the temple with copper axes, and the Gate of Peace was shattered with a pick axe. All the vessels of gold, silver, and copper were taken away from Nippur and sent to Akkad. Wisdom departed from Akkad and its good sense was turned to folly. And so the Guti, summoned by Enlil, attacked Akkad. "In less than five days, in less than ten days," the city was turned into a heap of ruins and disappeared from the face of the earth. War chariots and ships were destroyed. Robbers lurked by the roadside, the canals fell in, the fields produced no corn, there were no fish in the ponds. Many people died of starvation. And the gods of Sumer spoke the great curse over the city of Sargon and Naramsin: "O city that has dared to offend Enlil, you shall become as dust. Your bricks shall return to the abyss and your trees to the forest. The desert fox shall trail its brush over your ruins. Weeds shall overgrow the towpaths by your canals; along your highways only the 'wailing plant' shall grow, in your plains nothing but the 'reed of tears.' No man shall dare approach you for fear of mountain

*Stela of Naramsin, Susa, 3rd millenium* B.C. *(Paris)*

scorpions, snakes, and wild beasts. Instead of sweet water, bitter water shall flow through your land. And whoever says, 'I should like to live in this city' shall find no dwelling place here. Whoever says, 'I should like to lay me down to rest in Akkad' shall find no resting place there."

The curse of the Sumerian gods has indeed been fulfilled. Akkad has reverted to the desert and no one can say, even now, where the city of Sargon once stood.

The Akkadian kings were men of war. They razed many cities and subdued other nations. They sowed their seed in blood, and the harvest they reaped was their own annihilation. Under the barbarian rule of the Guti, for whom the Akkadians must take the responsibility, the temples fell into decay. The products of their workshops were crude and clumsy by comparison with those of earlier days, and the seals the Guti used to place their signature on clay tablets appear degenerate to us. But eventually there arose a prince of Uruk who rebelled against the "dragon from the mountains." He was able to kill the king of the Guti, who was deserted by his troops and fell into the hands of the victor, Utuchegal.

About the same time, an ensi, or governor, founded a new dynasty in Ur. At first he acknowledged the conqueror of the Guti as his overlord, but soon he himself took possession of the cities of Nippur and Kish and called himself king of Sumer and Akkad. The Semites who had produced such powerful warrior kings from their midst were pushed into the background once more.

In Lagash, the city of Eannatum, ruled another ensi who wanted nothing to do with war. He fixed his thoughts on building a new temple for Ningirsu and the other gods, and he wanted to be the good shepherd of his people, as the early Sumerian kings had been.

This prince of peace was named Gudea; which means "he who is summoned."

# Gudea, Builder of Temples

Lagash had suffered more than all the other Sumerian cities under the rule of Lugalzaggisi. The "man from Umma" had cut off the city's water supplies and destroyed its temples in order to drive away its guardian gods. For the governor of the stricken city, therefore, the building of a new temple had top priority. Then the canals had to be restored, the fields redistributed among the survivors and cultivated with greater energy than ever before. New trees had to be planted in place of those that had been felled.

Under the kings of Akkad, Lagash flourished once again. Then the "dragon from the mountains" brought fresh violence, but the city did not yield, and this time the gods stood by her. The rivers watered the fields without flooding them, the meadows flowered again, new canals and roads were constructed, new boats and carts were built, and new workshops were started. By the time Gudea became governor of Lagash, the number of its inhabitants had grown to two hundred and sixteen thousand.

No other Sumerian prince has left behind such extensive records of his work. On countless clay tablets and barrel-shaped bricks built into the foundations of his buildings, he accounted for his rule. He never called himself king, for he considered himself the steward of the god Ningirsu and he did not wish to be anything but the good shepherd of his people.

French archaeologists, first and foremost among them Ernest de Sarzec, found more than thirty statues representing Gudea.

In none of them does he carry arms, a war-club, or a scimitar. Humble yet self-assured, he either stands with folded hands, awaiting the commands of the god, or else he sits like a schoolboy, paying close attention to the words of the master. All the statues are made of enduring stone, and one of them shows him with the plan of a new temple on his knees. These statues were placed in temples that Gudea either built or restored, and recent excavations have proved that he was the greatest of all Sumerian temple builders.

He himself gives an account of how he came to build one of these temples: One day, the god of Lagash, Ningirsu, spoke to Gudea. "In my city is disorder. The flood waters of the Tigris do not rise as high as they should. The high waters do not glisten, they do not show their glory. The canals of Lagash do not carry enough good water to irrigate my fields." Gudea was wracked with doubt. In the night he dreamed, but he did not know what his dreams meant. He consulted Ningirsu: "You are the true prince of Lagash and I wish to carry out your commands, but what shall I do?" And to Baba, the divine queen of Lagash, he prayed: "You are the pure daughter of the heavens, through whom the land lives. You founded Lagash. The pious man whom you look on with favor will live long. I have no mother—you are my mother. In the sanctuary you gave me life. It is to my mother that I should like to tell my dreams. These dreams make me tremble and wake me with a start."

The goddess listened to the dreams that troubled Gudea so, and she sent him to another goddess, Nanshe, who knew the true meaning of all dreams. So Gudea went to Nanshe and addressed her: "In my dream there appeared before me a man with a god's crown. His head reached to the sky, his shoulders bore an eagle's wings, and his feet walked in the midst of a mighty wave. At his right hand there was a lion, and another at his left. I did not recognize him, but he commanded me to build a temple and then he disappeared. The sun rose and quickly climbed into the sky. Then a woman appeared holding a golden stylus. Who was she,

*Gudea carrying a palm frond, Telloh, 2200 B.C. (Paris)*

who was she not? She held a tablet and on it she drew the position of the stars in the sky. She took counsel with herself and then she vanished. Then I saw a man who drew a sketch of a temple on a tablet of lapis lazuli, and before him stood a wicker pannier and the mold of a brick filled with mud. And a he-ass stood by, pawing the ground with its hoof. Interpret this dream for me, Goddess, you who know the right meaning of dreams."

Then Nanshe spoke: "Gudea, you good shepherd, I will explain your dream to you. The man with the crown of a god and an eagle's wings, whose feet rise from a tidal wave, is my brother, Ningirsu. He commands you to build a new temple. The sun is your guardian god who rises from the earth in radiance. The woman with the golden stylus is the goddess Nisaba, who will see to it that the stars are in your favor while the temple is being built. The man with the lapis lazuli tablet is the god who will present you with the right plan for the temple building. But you, Gudea, are the he-ass with the pannier and the brick mold, and the pawing of its hoof shows how impatient you are to begin the building of the new temple. You will give the carpenters the timber they need; you will remove the seals from your treasury so that the craftsmen can fetch metals and precious stones from within. Through Ningirsu, who is as unfathomable as the skies, you will learn the correct design for the temple. He will guide you in your decisions."

Thereupon Gudea unsealed his treasury. He built a wagon to carry the precious things that were to adorn the temple. At the place of dread, the judgment seat of Ningirsu, Gudea sacrificed animals and burned sweet-smelling woods and he begged the god for a favorable sign. And Ningirsu gave him this promise: "On the day the good shepherd Gudea begins the rebuilding of the temple, the heavens will move over Lagash. A wind will come to herald the rain, and the rain will fall from heaven in abundance. The fields will yield rich harvests, the waters will rise in ditches and canals. In the land of Sumer, oil will flow abundantly and wool will be weighed out in plenty. On the day on which you start the restoration of my temple, I shall set my foot on the mountains whence comes the thunderstorm. And the wind I send shall breathe the breath of life into the land."

When Ningirsu had pronounced these good words, he gave Gudea the exact measurements for the temple and Gudea drew them on a tablet. Then the site was cleared of thorns and weeds. Boats and caravans of asses were sent forth and they brought back precious timber from the eastern mountains, marble and limestone blocks from the mountains in the west, gold dust from Nubia, copper from the Euphrates, sweet-smelling woods from the island of Dilmun, and diorite from Arabia. Everything was heaped into new storehouses, and in the spice room the stocks of spices rose like the waters of the Tigris. In the treasury articles made of precious stones, of metals and of lead were piled high.

Then the building began. Like a young man who builds a

house for himself, Gudea could think of nothing else. He was like a man who forgets to eat and drink. The whole nation helped with the building, and even Elamites and Egyptians came from their countries to assist in the work. At last the new temple stood there, shining like the sun among the stars, like a hill of lapis lazuli, like a mountain of marble. Everyone was lost in admiration and Gudea placed statues inside, and decorated the interior with golden lamps and vessels.

And just as Gudea had cleared the site of weeds, so did he rid the land of the magicians who had kept the people in fear. In the new temple Gudea reintroduced the Holy Wedding of Dumuzi and Inanna, so that the Feast of the New Year should be celebrated once more as in the ancient days. For seven whole days all disputes were set aside. The hungry sat down to eat at the tables of the rich. No angry words were spoken, the weak were not beaten, and no poor man could have his goods seized for debt. No man might insult another, and master and slave, mistress and slave-girl were all considered equal. For seven nights in the city of Lagash, the high and the low slept side by side.

So it says in the records that Gudea left for future generations. There is no doubt that under his governorship magnificent buildings were erected in Lagash. In his reign it was a wealthy city. These riches, however, were not amassed in war nor by forceable seizure in predatory raids, but because a prince of peace inspired his subjects to perform great works of peace. Under Gudea, the relationship between gods and men that had prevailed "at the beginning of time" was re-established. This true king, who never called himself a king, whose likeness was depicted carrying a palm branch instead of a sword, was one whom the people served with greater devotion than ever they had rendered to the conqueror Eannatum. The Sumerians were tired of war. And their rulers everywhere concentrated on the Sumerian way of life. The Akkadians were not oppressed in the process, however. On the contrary, one of the kings of Ur built a great wall to protect Akkadian cities against the attacks of the Amorites.

It was not only the temples that were restored but also the rule of law. Urnammu, the founder of the third dynasty of Ur, whose five kings secured a century of peace for the Land of Sumer, not only gave the ziggurat of his town a new form, he also improved the laws and had them engraved on clay tablets and blocks of stone. These stelae were set up in public places for the benefit of the people. Any man with a grievance could stand before them and the inscription would explain to him what were his rights, "so that he found justice and his heart could sigh with relief."

In 1952, Professor Kramer was working in the Museum of the Ancient Orient in Istanbul when he found what is, so far, the oldest known code of laws, inscribed on a tablet that had been written on Urnammu's orders. The introduction says that after the creation of the world, Anu, the god of the skies, and Enlil, god of the earth, entrusted the city of Ur to the moon-god. When Urnammu became king of Ur, the moon-god ordered him to re-establish the old order that had been destroyed by war. And Urnammu drove out the evildoers and those who had come into possession of oxen, sheep, and asses by swindling the farmers of Ur. He had the balance and weights tested, and he saw to it that the man with one shekel was not exploited by the man with sixty shekels. Urnammu reintroduced the old laws so that justice should prevail, and no man found himself at the mercy of arbitrary decisions or individual caprice.

There followed a list of rules under which judgment was to be pronounced in Ur. If a man disowned his mother, he was to have his hair cut off, be led round the town, and then expelled. The compensations for injuries were laid down precisely. This was not the harsh code of an "eye for an eye and a tooth for a tooth," but followed more humane principles. Urnammu took pains to see that the overambitious found their master; and once a man had paid for his crime, forgiveness must follow. The enemy, too,

*Section of Urnammu stela, Ur, 2200 B.C. (Philadelphia)*

must be dealt with justly and on one Sumerian tablet there is even the sentence: "Repay evil with good."

For the poor it was no longer a case of "hunger is their food." Everyone, even the highest in the land, had to serve. The kings set a good example. There is a stela over three feet high on which Urnammu is represented several times, but always in the same way, that is, as a man eager to do the service of the gods. The illustrations are carefully arranged in bands, like the friezes on the alabaster vase from Uruk, which is a thousand years older. On this stela, men are vying with each other to pay honor to the gods. Unfortunately, large portions have been destroyed, but one remaining strip shows the king working side by side with bricklayers to build the temple walls. In the top register, Urnammu is being installed as the true king of Ur, and his patron god, the moon-god, is handing him the judgment staff and measuring tape, the symbols of justice. In a third picture, the king has shouldered so many builder's tools that one man, most concerned, is hastening to his aid.

Urnammu and Gudea introduced an era of peace into Sumer. There is no sharper contrast to the statues of Gudea than one of Entemena, who called himself the king of Lagash, and who often waged war. The head of this statue is missing and the stump of the neck has been polished smooth by the numbers of hands that have passed over it. Obviously it was erected by Entemena for his glorification, but it had been carried off, beheaded, and placed on show, to make the former conqueror of Umma an object of scorn. The statues of Gudea and the stelae of Urnammu were spared such a fate. As they refused to sow violence, they reaped not hatred but admiration, even from those who came thousands of years later.

# The Winged Horse

About 2000 B.C., the Land of Sumer was invaded by warlike hordes from the east and west. From the east came the Elamites and from the west, the Amorites. They wished to seize power in the fertile land between the rivers that had been turned into a huge garden. The Elamites settled in the old city of the sun-god, Larsa, the Amorites in Isin, which is at the same height as Nippur, the city of Enlil. One Sumerian city after another cracked in the pincer movement that gripped the land.

Ibissin, the last king of Ur whose name is still cited as king of all Sumer, defended himself desperately against the overwhelming attack. The Semitic tribesmen from the west could not be halted. When Larsa, too, fell into their hands, the Elamites had to withdraw again, and Ibissin fled to Susa with them. In Nippur, the prince of Mari was declared king of Sumer by the priests of Enlil, and the Sumerian line of kings that had lasted for one thousand years came to an end.

The chronicler laments the event in these words: "The days of the great rulers are over. Shattered are the cities, and the people slain. Sumer is overwhelmed by the flood of its enemies. The gods have withdrawn. The goddess has abandoned her shrine. There is no one left to hear the cry for help. Woe, my city! Woe, my house! The Black-headed People no longer celebrate their feasts, the white radiance of the festive robes of the priesthood is nowhere to be seen. The sheepfolds are laid waste, the cattle stalls are destroyed. The royal throne now stands on foreign soil. Where can a fair judgment be found now? To Elam the king has fled, like a bird whose nest is destroyed, and Sumer has become a land of fear, a land of death."

As in the days after the invasion of the Guti, the cities were devastated and many men were killed. But defeat did not mean the end. Sumer lasted longer than the furious dragon from the mountains. And the conquerors from the west observed the defeated closely. The Amorites did indeed seize power, but as soon as they had consolidated their rule, there came a period when the Sumerians could once more live the lives they were accustomed to. Yes, the conquerors learned much from the Sumerians. The soldiers became pupils, and they soon showed that they were gifted ones and able to learn quickly.

The struggles between east and west continued. One king of Elam attacked Larsa and drove out the ruler. The son of the conqueror, who became king of Ur, was so deeply impressed by Sumerian buildings, statues, and inscriptions that he did all he could to preserve them. The kings who followed him also "raised the head of Sumer." The fame of the Land of Ur spread in all directions. Sumerian doctors and astronomers, architects, and sculptors, cutters of seals and scribes became teachers in other lands.

The Sumerian gods lived on, too, although other nations gave them different names. Inanna became the goddess Ishtar, Enki grew into Ea, and Utu developed into Shamash. The epics of the Babylonians, Assyrians, Hittites, and Hurrites incorporated Sumerian kings and heroes like Utnapishtim, who found eternal life, and Gilgamesh, who sought it. And if the Sumerians no longer supplied the ruling dynasties in the Land of the Two Rivers, the new kings abided by the laws that the Sumerian monarchs had laid down. Year by year, at the Feast of the New Year, the Holy Wedding continued to be celebrated to ensure the rebirth of nature throughout the land. Year after year the custom was followed whereby the king handed over his power to a man of the people, and made himself the servant of all others. How seriously this custom was taken is shown by what happened some two hundred years after the flight of Ibissin.

A king of the west Semite dynasty of Isin appointed his gardener as the "Seven-Day-King," but while the celebrations were in progress the real king died suddenly. And then an astonishing thing happened. The people rallied behind the gardener who wore the crown for the moment and, according to ancient custom, he was confirmed in his high office. As the gods had summoned the old king "in the days of his humility," no one, not even the royal heir, was allowed to dispute the gardener's right to the throne.

The gardener-king actually reigned for twenty-four years. As it says in the ancient chronicle, he spread "light over Isin and other cities." He called himself "the chosen of Inanna."

Sumer had ceased to exist, yet the conquerors of Sumer continued to behave and live like Sumerians.

Fifteen hundred years later, one of the kings who reigned over the Land of the Two Rivers had a collection made of everything he could find that had been written about the Sumerians. Ashburbanipal, terrible in war, "learned to read Sumerian in the intricate tablets." Many collections of old inscriptions were preserved in Assyrian times. An American scholar found a jug in Nippur in which were the records from seventeen centuries— a whole library in one jug! On one clay tablet, there was found a sketch plan of the city of Nippur itself. It was so accurate that it could be used as a guide for the further excavation of the city in the middle of the twentieth century.

Thanks to the work of dedicated scholars over the past hundred years, we know more today about the beginnings of civilization in the Land of the Two Rivers than did Ashurbanipal. Through excavation, the earliest periods of man's history have been brought back to life. Botta and Layard and Rassam were entitled to believe that they had come upon the "original" palaces in the mounds of Nimrud and Kuyunjik, but it soon became clear that these first explorers had hardly reached the days of the Biblical kings. British, French, German, American, Turkish, Italian, Japanese, Danish and Iraqi archaeologists have extracted find after find from the earth and exposed foundation after foundation, and they went on digging down to the virgin soil on which the very first settlers began to build. But when that was cannot yet be stated with any degree of certainty. Even now we do not know when Sumer began.

In the Land of the Two Rivers, another Holy Wedding was celebrated continually, the union between the various peoples. Immigrants from the east mingled with the first settlers and learned from them. The Semites, invading from the west, adopted Sumerian fashions and then handed them on to other nations. The Land of Ur was a school where many subjects were taught. Here one could learn how to write on tablets of clay, to cut seals in stone, to observe the stars, to make out prescriptions, to tame rivers, and to dig canals that controlled flooding, to keep back the encroachments of the desert.

To preserve the paradise so laboriously created, to bolt the door against mortality, these were the aims of all the Sumerian

*Winged horse with foal, fighting a lion.*
*Cylinder-seal impression, 1400 B.C. (after Southesk)*

kings. They tried to put them into effect, each in his different fashion. Gilgamesh made his protest against dying. Etana flew to heaven to try to bring the herb of easy childbirth down to earth. The kings of the first dynasty of Ur took all their retinue with them into the grave, so convinced were they of their immortality. Gudea and other princes of peace built temples and statues whose dignity has lasting value. But the influence of the Sumerians has been strongest through the great poems they wrote on clay tablets in cuneiform script.

The Greeks used to say that the fountain of poesy sprang from the ground when the winged-horse Pegasus struck the earth with its hoof. In the Land of the Two Rivers, pictures of the winged horse have been found more than once. On one seal, it is defending its foal, whose wings are not yet formed, against a lion. It is hard to think of any more moving representation of the triumph over the threat of death and violence.

From every century of Sumerian life, we have inherited something that excites our admiration. But the songs and epics of the people of the Land of Ur set a pattern for posterity throughout the world.

## WORDS, PLACES, AND PEOPLE

*Adab*  Sumerian city, southeast of Nippur, capital of the ninth dynasty "after the Flood," according to the Sumerian king-lists. Now called Bismaya.

*Adad*  Akkadian god of the weather.

*Agrab*  Mound of ruins in the Diyala region. Important American excavation here in 1936–37.

*Akkad*  Capital of the Akkadian empire founded by Sargon, destroyed by the Guti. The site has not yet been identified. Also called Agade.

*Alabaster*  Stone containing lime or gypsum, often translucent, widely used for making statues and vessels.

*Al Ubaid*  Important mound of ruins near Ur.

*Amazonite*  Green semiprecious stone.

*Amorites*  Old name for a western Semitic tribe from Amor (Amurru), who came from the middle reaches of the Euphrates and the Syrian desert.

*Anu*  Sumerian-Akkadian god of the skies whose main shrine was at Uruk.

*Apsu*  "The watery deeps" ruled by the god Enki. The Sumerians also made offerings to him in wells and via drainage shafts.

*Ashur*  One of the great cities of the Assyrian empire, situated on the right bank of the Tigris. It was discovered at Qalat Shergat and excavated by Walter Andrae between 1903 and 1936.

*Ashurbanipal* King of Assyria (668–631 B.C.). His famous palace and library were excavated at Kuyunjik by Layard, Rassam, and Loftus.

*Asmar (Tell)* Mound in the Diyala region, site of the old city of Eshnunna, excavated by the Americans under H. Frankfort.

*Assyria* Country on the upper Tigris, whose chief cities were Ashur, Calah, Nineveh, and Dur Sharrukin.

*Assyrians* A warlike race who overthrew the Babylonians.

*Babylon* Capital of old Mesopotamia at the time of Hammurabi (1792–1750 B.C.).

*Babylonia* Country between the Euphrates and the Tigris south of Assyria.

*Basalt* Gray, black-veined volcanic stone, used for sculpture in Mesopotamia.

*Bilalama* King of Eshnunna, believed to be the author of a code of laws that was only recorded one hundred years after his death.

*Bismaya* Mound in which the Sumerian city of Adab was discovered.

*Black-headed People* The name by which the Sumerians referred to themselves.

*Brak (Tell)* Mound in the Habur valley, excavated by Mallowan 1937–39.

*Calah* An Assyrian palace excavated by Layard and Mallowan at Nimrud.

*Cuneiform* A Mesopotamian script whose wedge-shaped signs were made by impressing a stylus on a smooth surface of moist clay.

*Cylinder seal* An engraved seal like a slim cotton reel, usually with a hole bored through the middle. It was rolled in wet clay to leave an impression.

*Diorite* Hard volcanic stone, blue-black in color, imported into Mesopotamia chiefly from Arabia and Nubia.

*Diyala*   Left-hand tributary of the Tigris. Its important excavation sites include Agrab, Asmar, and Khafajah.

*Dumuzi*   Shepherd-god and king of the first dynasty of Uruk, husband of the goddess Inanna.

*Dur Sharrukin*   "The Citadel of Sargon," the Assyrian palace discovered in the mound of Khorsabad.

*E-anna*   "The house of Heaven," chief shrine of the god Anu in Uruk.

*Eannatum*   King of Lagash, *c.* 2700 B.C. Famous for The Stela of the Vultures, set up in his honor.

*Eden*   Sumerian word meaning "steppe."

*Elam*   Old name for region of Iran lying east of Mesopotamia.

*Enki*   Sumerian god of wisdom, "lord of the watery deeps," whose city was Eridu.

*Enkidu*   The friend of Gilgamesh.

*Enlil*   God of the earth and the winds, whose city was Nippur and who decided who should hold the kingship of Sumer.

*Ensi*   City governor, both prince and high priest, viceroy of the patron god of the city.

*Entemena*   Ensi of Lagash, involved in a war of rivalry with the city of Umma.

*Erech*   Biblical name for Uruk, discovered in the mound of Warka.

*Eridu*   The oldest Sumerian city yet discovered. It was concealed in the mound of Abu Shahrein. Originally it stood by a freshwater lagoon and was the city of the god Enki.

*Etana*   Shepherd-king of the first dynasty of Kish. He mounted aloft on an eagle's back to fetch the herb of easy childbirth for humanity, but gave up the attempt when the earth threatened to disappear from sight.

*Euphrates*   The "copper river," one of the two arteries of Mesopotamia.

*Fara* Ruins of the Sumerian city of Shuruppak, the home of Utnapishtim, who built an ark and so survived the Flood. Excavated by Koldewey and Andrae.

*Gilgamesh* King of Uruk who overcame wild beasts and monsters and built the walls around Uruk; the most famous Mesopotamian hero.

*Gudea* The greatest governor of Lagash—temple builder and the "good shepherd."

*Guti* A barbaric mountain tribe who attacked Sumer from the north, overthrew the Akkadian dynasty and remained dominant for a hundred years.

*Habur* Left-hand tributary of the Euphrates.

*Hammurabi* Founder of the first dynasty of Babylon (1792–1750 B.C.); renowned for the stela inscribed with his code of laws, found in Susa.

*Hariri* Ruined remains of Mari, an ancient kingdom on the middle Euphrates with a magnificent palace. Excavated by the French under André Parrot.

*Hassuna (Tell)* Mound near Nineveh, with an ancient settlement excavated by Iraqi archaeologists.

*Imdugud* Lion-headed eagle, personifying the god Ningirsu.

*Inanna* Goddess with chief temple in Uruk, known as Ishtar by the Babylonians.

*Isin* Sumerian capital of a western Semitic dynasty, found in the mound of Ishan Bahrije.

*Jemdet Nasr* Important excavation site northeast of Kish. It gives its name to an early phase of ancient Mesopotamian culture, the period about the turn of the fourth/third millennia B.C.

*Ka'lat Jarmo* Village in Mesopotamia with evidence of settlements from as long ago as *c.* 5000 B.C.

*Khafajah* Ruins in the Diyala region, excavated by the Americans.

*Khorsabad* Mound where Botta discovered the palace of Sargon II (721–705 B.C.) in 1843, the old city of Dur Sharrukin.

*Kuyunjik* Mound on the left bank of the Tigris where Nineveh was found. Famous for the palaces of Sennacherib and Ashurbanipal. An ancient foundation with a sequence of strata nearly one hundred feet thick.

*Lagash* Sumerian city discovered in the hill of Telloh by Sarzec and other French archaeologists.

*Lapis lazuli* Azure-blue semiprecious stone, imported into Mesopotamia from Media, used for mosaics and jewelry.

*Larsa* Palace of western Semitic dynasty, conquered by Hammurabi, discovered in the mound of Senkere.

*Lugal* Sumerian term for king: literally "great man."

*Lugalzaggisi* King of the third dynasty of Uruk, *c.* 2500 B.C., who destroyed Lagash. He conquered an extensive empire, but was defeated by Sargon.

*Mari* Palace of the tenth dynasty "after the Flood," situated on the middle Euphrates.

*Mesannepadda* King of the first dynasty of Ur, proved to have been a real king by the discovery of a foundation tablet in Al Ubaid. Perhaps identifiable with Mesilim of Kish.

*Mesopotamia* The Land of the Two Rivers, lying between the Euphrates and the Tigris. It was never a precise geographical entity but it corresponds more or less to present day Iraq.

*Mina* Babylonian term for a unit of weight, approximately one pound (500 gr).

*Muallafat* Arabic name for the oldest settlement yet discovered in Mesopotamia.

*Muqayyar* Mound in which Ur was discovered. The Arabic name means "hill of pitch" because remains of asphalt were found there.

*Nannar* The Sumerian moon-god, worshiped in Ur.

*Naramsin*   Important monarch, grandson of Sargon (*c.* 2300 B.C.).

*Nimrud*   Mound where Layard discovered the Assyrian palace of Calah.

*Ningirsu*   Patron god of Lagash.

*Nineveh*   One of the chief cities of Assyria on the upper Tigris.

*Ninsun*   Goddess, mother of Gilgamesh.

*Nippur*   Sumerian city, discovered in the hill of Nuffar, whose patron god was Enlil.

*Onager*   Wild ass, used as a draft animal in ancient Mesopotamia.

*Picture-writing* (*or pictographs*)   The oldest form of written communication. From this developed the cuneiform script of the Mesopotamians and the hieroglyphs of the Egyptians. The earliest examples come from Kish, Uruk, and Jemdet Nasr, and date from the end of the fourth millenium B.C. They were inscribed on stone and on clay.

*Sennacherib*   Assyrian king (704–681 B.C.) who destroyed Babylon.

*Sarbatu tree*   Planted in Mesopotamia to shade young plants and to act as windbreaks.

*Sargon*   Founder of the dynasty of Akkad (2360–2304 B.C.).

*Sargon II*   Ruled in Dur Sharrukin (721–705 B.C.), king of Assyria.

*Semites*   Racial group, probably originally from the Arabian peninsula.

*Shamash*   Akkadian name for the Sumerian sun-god Utu.

*Sharkalisharri*   "King of Kings," fifth king of the dynasty of Akkad.

*Shekel*   Babylonian term for the smallest Sumerian coin and weight: 1 shekel = $\frac{1}{60}$ mina = $\frac{1}{3600}$ talent: approximately $\frac{1}{4}$ oz. or 8.4 gr.

*Shuruppak*   The city of Utnapishtim found in the hill of Fara. Utnapishtim is identified with the Sumerian Ziusudra who built an ark and so survived the Flood.

*Sippar*  Sumerian city dedicated to the sun-god Utu. It was discovered in the mound of Abu Habba, and Akkad may eventually be traced in this area.

*Stela (or stele)*  Upright monument, usually carved with reliefs and inscriptions.

*Subartu*  Northern Mesopotamia, roughly the area known later as Assyria.

*Sumer*  The land between Kish and Eridu.

*Sumerians*  A people who settled in the Land of the Two Rivers about the middle of the fourth millennium B.C., having migrated from the east.

*Susa*  Ancient city in southeast Iran, excavated by the French since 1897.

*Tell*  Arabic term for mound of ruins.

*Telloh*  Site from which Lagash was excavated, also known as Tell Lot.

*Tigris*  The more easterly of the twin rivers, once known as Idiglat, which means the "arrow swift."

*Umma*  Sumerian city, rival of Lagash, found in the mound of Jocha.

*Ur*  Sumerian city discovered in the mound of Muqayyar, excavated by Sir Leonard Woolley, 1922–34.

*Urnammu*  Founder of the third dynasty of Ur, a great builder and lawgiver.

*Uruk*  Sumerian city capital of King Gilgamesh, discovered in the mound of Warka.

*Utu*  The sun-god of the Sumerians.

*Vultures, the Stela of the*  Monument erected by Eannatum, king of Lagash, after defeating the city of Umma.

*Wall-cone mosaic*  A technique from early Sumerian times, whereby finger-length clay pegs with colored heads were driven into the plaster coating of walls and pillars to make decorative patterns.

*Zagros*  Mountain range to the north of Mesopotamia, home of the Guti who attacked the Akkadians, destroyed their kingdom, and dominated most of Mesopotamia for a hundred years.

*Ziggurat*  A stepped or terraced tower with a temple at the top, and a reception ramp for the gods to descend to earth.

*Ziusudra*  King of Shuruppak, the last of the ten most ancient rulers of old Mesopotamia. The Babylonians called him Utnapishtim. He is said to have built an ark and thus survived the Flood.

## FAMOUS MESOPOTAMIAN EXPLORERS

*Andrae, Walter* (1875–1936). Pupil of Koldewey, excavated Ashur.

*Botta, Paul-Émile* (1802–1870). French consul, discovered Khorsabad, one of the pioneers.

*Chiera, Edward* (1855–1933). American Assyriologist and excavator.

*Flandin, Eugene* (1809–1876). French artist, who helped Botta at the first excavation of Khorsabad.

*Frankfort, Henry* (1897–1954). American archaeologist.

*Jordan, Julius* (1878–1945). Pupil of Koldewey, excavated Uruk.

*Koldewey, R. J.* (1855–1925). German excavator of Babylon.

*Langdon, H. St.* (1876–1937). British Assyriologist, led excavations in Kish and Jemdet Nasr.

*Parrot, André.* French archaeologist, excavated Mari.

*Smith, George* (1840–1876). British Assyriologist, discovered the story of the Flood.

*Layard, Sir Austen Henry* (1817–1894). Pioneered the excavation of Nineveh, Calah, Nimrud, Babylon, Ashur and Kish.

*Loftus, Sir William Kennet.* British excavator who, in the mid-nineteenth century, explored Susa, Nippur, Uruk, Ur, Eridu, Nineveh, and Nimrud.

*Mallowan, M. E. L.* Contemporary British archaeologist, has excavated in Nineveh, Tell Brak, Nimrud, and Balawat.

*Moortgat, Anton* (b. 1897). German orientalist and excavator.

*Morgan, Jacques de* (1857–1924). Excavated Susa.

*Noldecke, A.* excavated in Uruk 1931–39.

*Oppenheim, Max von.* explored Tell Halaf.

*Place, Victor* (1818–1875). French excavator of Khorsabad. Most of his finds sank in the Tigris.

*Rassam, Hormuzd* (1826–1910). Christian Chaldaean, successful excavator.

*Rawlinson, Sir Henry Creswicke* (1810–95). The British "father of Assyriology."

*Sarzec, Ernest de* (1837–1901). Frenchman who excavated Telloh (Lagash).

*Schmidt* (b. 1897). American archaeologist.

*Taylor, J. E.* British consul, dug in Ur, 1854–55.

*Thompson, R. Campbell* (1876–1941). British Assyriologist, dug in Nineveh, Eridu, etc.

*Thureau-Dangin, François* (1872–1944). French Assyriologist and excavator.

*Wooley, Sir Leonard* (1880–1960). British archaeologist, excavated Ur 1922–39.

## MAJOR EXCAVATIONS IN CHRONOLOGICAL ORDER

1844 Botta begins search for Nineveh, digs first in Kuyunjik: 1843–44 in Khorsabad. On May 1, 1847, the Louvre opens an Assyrian room.

1845 Layard makes important finds in Nineveh, Nimrud, and Ashur.

1852 Place and Fresnel dig in Nineveh and Babylon. On May 21, 1855, large crates of finds are waylaid near Corna and most of them sink in the Tigris.

1853 Rawlinson, Rassam, Loftus, Taylor, start work on excavation sites of which no more was known than their Arabic names: Warka (Uruk), Senkere (Larsa), Muqayyar (Ur), Abu Shahrein (Eridu).

1854 Loftus finds early peg mosaics in Uruk, draws sketch maps of cities of Uruk and Susa.

1857 Rawlinson, Hincks, and Oppert prove by simultaneous translations of the same text that they have succeeded in deciphering cuneiform.

1877 Sarzec discovers Lagash and makes many finds.

1887 Koldewey digs at Telloh; in 1899 the methodical exploration of Babylon begins.

1889 Americans begin to dig in Nippur.

1885–90 British teams dig at many places in Assyria.

1903 Andrae, in Ashur, develops an excavation technique for sorting out the complications when various strata are superimposed. He puts it to excellent use.

1912   Oppenheim digs in Tell Halaf.

1918–39   "The Golden Age" of oriental archaeology.

1918   Thompson digs in Ur.

1919   Hall digs in Ur.

1922   Woolley begins his twelve year task at Ur. In 1927–29 he excavates the Royal Graves.

1923–33   British and Americans, led by Langdon, dig in Kish. The Jemdet Nasr phase is recognized.

1928   German archaeologists resume the excavations begun in 1913. Strata from the fifth millenium B.C. are exposed.

1929   French excavators return to Telloh.

1930   Frankfort leads American excavations in Asmar, Khafajah, Agrab, and Ishali. Chiera, Pfeiffer, Starr, Bache, and Delougaz also take part later.

1934   Parrot begins to dig at Mari.

1946   Iraqi archaeologists dig at Eridu.

1948   Americans dig at Nippur.

1952   Mallowan digs at Nimrud. At present there are French, American, British, Iraqi, and German teams at work in Mesopotamia.

CHRONOLOGICAL TABLE WITH NAMES OF KINGS

According to the Babylonian king-lists, ten kings of antiquity reigned in Mesopotamia before the Flood. Ziusudra of Shuruppak was the last of these, and he built an ark and so survived the Flood. After the Flood there were twenty-three kings of the first dynasty of Kish, including Etana, "the shepherd." Then followed the first dynasty of Uruk with twelve kings, including Enmerkar, Dumuzi, and Gilgamesh.

For the period prior to 2000 B.C., which is the one covered by this book, the dating is still a subject of controversy. The dates below steer a middle course between the two extremes suggested by experts. The following broad classifications are used to cover the most ancient periods of prehistory:

| | |
|---|---|
| 5000–4500 | Jarmo Period |
| 4500–4000 | Hassuna Period (neolithic) |
| 4000–3500 | Tell Halaf Period (stone-copper age) |
| 3500–3200 | Al 'Ubaid Period (copper-stone age) |
| 3200–3000 | Uruk Period |
| 3000–2600 | Jemdet Nasr Period |
| 2600–2500 | Mesilim Period |

Then come the following dynasties with historically verified kings:

2500–2380  First dynasty of Ur, including kings Mesannepadda, Aannapadda, Urnanshe, Eannatum, Ennanatum I, Entenema, Ennanatum II, Lugalanda, Urukagina.

2380–2360  The third dynasty of Uruk, with kings Lugalzaggisi (of Umma) and Urzababa (of Kish).

2360–2260  Dynasty of Akkad with kings Sargon (2360–2304), Rimush, Manishtusu, Naramsin, and Sharkalisharri.

2260–2150  Guti conquest with twenty-one kings.

2150–2130  Fifth dynasty of Uruk with King Utuchengal.

2140–2100  Gudea of Lagash.

2124–2016  Third dynasty of Ur with kings Urnammu (2124–2107), Shulgi (2106–2059), Amursin (2058–2050), Shusin (2049–2040), Ibissin (2040–2016).

With the third dynasty of Ur, which was overthrown by the Amorites, the kingdom of Sumer comes to an end.

SOURCES FOR THE COLOR PLATES

Boudot-Lamotte, Paris: 6 and 7

Dr. Ludwig Delp, Munich: 2 above and below, 8 above and below, 18, 19 above and below

Hirmer, Munich: 1, 4 below, 5, 10, 11, 13, 15, 16 as well as front jacket (Two dignitaries, fresco from the ruins of Barsip, circa 740 B.C., Aleppo) and back jacket (Ziggurat of Aqar Quf, circa 1350 B.C.)

Holle-Archiv, Baden-Baden: 4 above, 9, 12, 14, 17, 20 and 24

Vorderasiatisches Museum, Berlin: 3

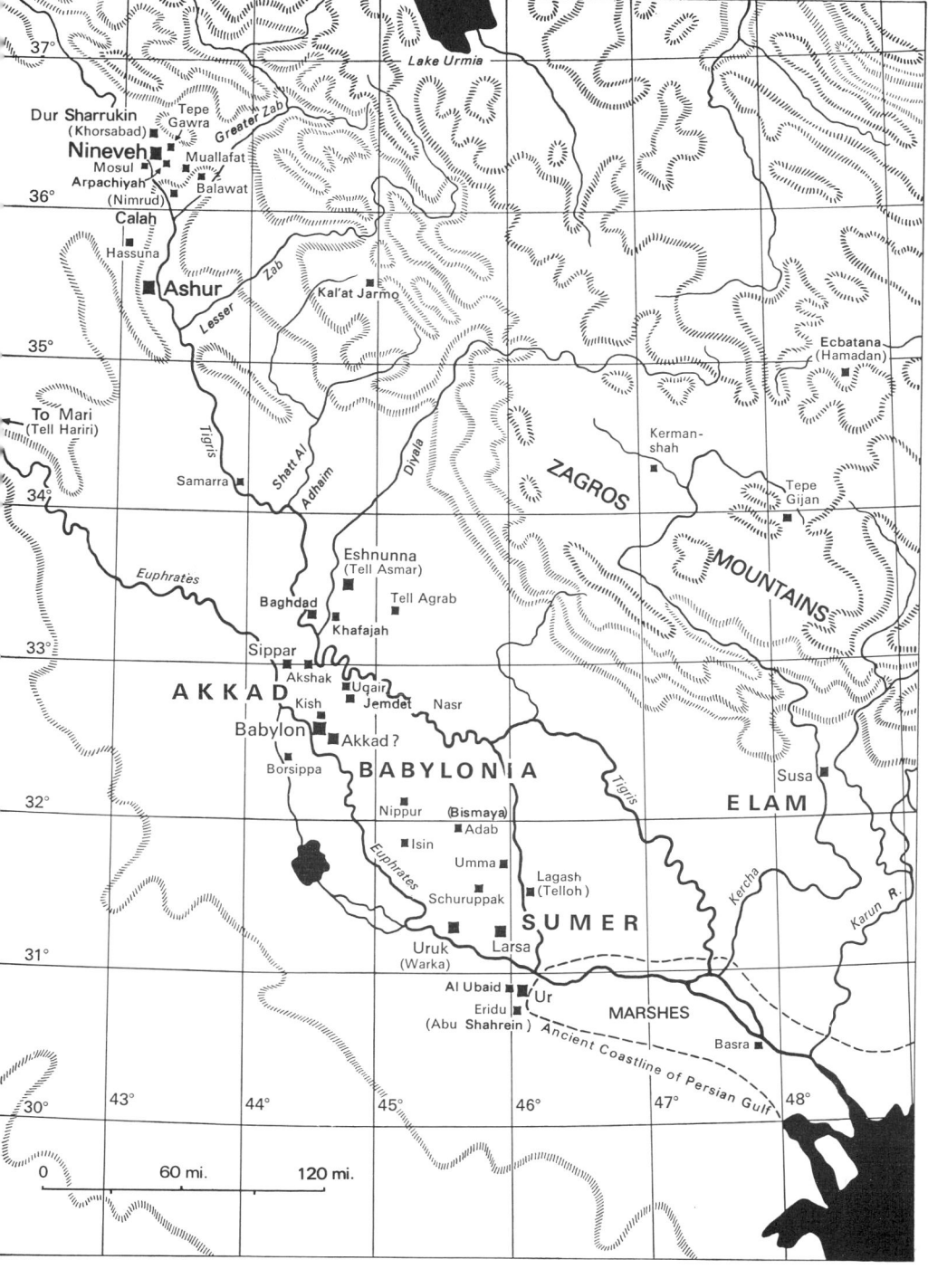